# Truth for Our Youth

*A Self-Empowerment Book for Teens*

Agyei Tyehimba

Copyright © 2014 Agyei Tyehimba

All rights reserved.

ISBN: 1497420431
ISBN-13: 978-1497420434

# DEDICATION

This book, and its spirit, energy and ideas, is dedicated first to my daughters Nubia and Zakiya whom I love dearly. You're both bright, beautiful, talented, and raised on many of the principles in this book. Words cannot express how proud I am of you; Second, I dedicate this book to the young people pictured on the cover of my book. I once taught all of these young people when they were fifth-eighth grade students at the school I helped to create called KAPPA M.S. 215 in the Bronx, New York back in 2000. Many of them are now college graduates. They are proof of what can happen when our children receive a thorough education in a safe and positive environment from people who love and value them; Third, I dedicate this book to all youth in America. I have great love for you and faith that you will be better and do better than my generation. I believe this society must do more to empower youth, especially youth of color. Contrary to what you've been told, you ARE something, can be something, and can have something....But you must believe in yourself, then develop yourself and help others do the same.

## TABLE OF CONTENTS

*Dedication iii*

*Acknowledgements i*

# PART I: FOR TEENS

*Introduction: Get Ready to Fly! 3*

*The Greatest Love of All 15*

*Play Chess, Not Checkers 45*

*Social Etiquette: Don't Leave Home Without It 67*

*Message for Black Youth Around the World 79*

*Invest in Yourself 97*

*Managing Peer Pressure 113*

*AVOID the Traps! 125*

*Tips for Managing Your Time 147*

*How to Choose Friends Wisely 161*

*Conclusion 172*

# PART II: FOR PARENTS

*The Wizard of Oz Syndrome 181*

*The Education of Black and Brown Children 191*

| *Expanding our Thinking About Parenting 205* |
| *Unlocking Your Child's Intelligence and Ability 211* |
| *9 Things We Shouldn't Teach our Children 219* |
| *About the Author 228* |

# ACKNOWLEDGMENTS

I'd like to acknowledge people/institutions in and out of my community of Harlem, NY that extended themselves to me during my adolescent and young adult years. Their encouragement and mentorship guided me to become an empowered, clear-thinking, and free-thinking adult. Some are still alive while others have transitioned to the world of ancestors. I am eternally grateful for them all: My 143$^{rd}$ Street peeps like Shelby, Spencer, and Dwayne "Rope Ditty" Roper, Convent Avenue Baptist Church, the Baptist Youth Fellowship and many caring adults at Convent (Mrs. Virgina Griffin, Ms. Barbara Perkins, Irene Farrah, Reverend James Logan, Deacon Pearson, Sarah & Denise) Marie Brown, and many more. I cannot forget my parents and grandparents who were my first and most important mentors! I humbly thank you all. I repay you by doing my best to give youth today what you gave me, because *it saved my life.*

# PART I

# For Teens

# INTRODUCTION: GET READY TO FLY!

*A journey of a thousand miles begins with a single step.*

*Lao-Tzu*

Congratulations, my young reader! Whether you purchased this book yourself, or someone else did, you are reading it, which means you care about your life and you are interested in gaining respect, success, and power.

Many so-called experts have counted you out. They believe yours is a lost and hopeless generation. By reading this book, you are well on your way to proving them wrong.

## DON'T BELIEVE THE HYPE!

I'm sure you've heard it all before:

- ✓ "Kids had respect for themselves and others when I was growing up."

- ✓ "These young people today don't know how to act."

- ✓ "If it's not on television or in a song, these kids don't know about it."

- ✓ "Babies having babies, gangbanging, and jail….They're lost and confused."

- ✓ "His/her father was a loser and he will be one too….the apple doesn't fall far from the tree."

These negative comments about teenagers appear in magazines, newspapers, talk shows, and street corner gossip. Let's be honest. Some youth in America have attitudes and behavior that support these statements! But this does not apply to <u>all</u> youth.

Many of you are basically good people in need of direction. If you allow yourself to believe you are destined to fail, you will also believe that the future holds little hope for you and your friends. Or you might believe that you have no real control over your life. Your family background, race, neighborhood, and income level predetermine your fate, right? Wrong! You are about to learn simple yet powerful ideas that will teach you how to take control of your life regardless of what your circumstances are.

As an adolescent, you probably have many concerns and obstacles. You want to be independent, yet you feel confined by your parents' rules. You attend school but have no idea how this will really help you later in life. Friends, dating, earning money, and choosing a future career may be important to you right now, but you don't know where to begin. Then there's the pressure of living up to your parents and teachers expectations.

If any of this applies to you, don't feel bad. Your parents and their parents faced many of the same concerns and challenges you face now. Most adults, including myself, would like to think that we were so different in our youth from teenagers today. The truth is that we were just like you in many ways.

Some adults that are successful and confident now, came from broken homes and neighborhoods that were poor and violent. Some of us lacked confidence in ourselves and were not very popular. We were confused about what we wanted to do with our lives, and didn't see ourselves being successful in the future. Some of us joined gangs, dropped out of school, and made other bad decisions. Yet we still made it. How, you ask? Maybe we had strong parents that taught us good habits and values. Or maybe we had neighbors or teachers that took a special interest in us, and provided us with guidance and exposed us to new things. Show me a respected and successful adult, and I'll show you someone that received guidance and support from *somewhere or someone*. None of us became successful by ourselves.

Take me for example. Now, I'm a father, educator, activist, and published writer. But I didn't have it easy as a teenager. I grew up in the famed neighborhood of Harlem, New York during the turbulent 80's.

Several gangs turned sections of the city into violent battle zones. Crack cocaine first made its debut, turning thousands of people into addicts, thieves and prostitutes. Subway crime, street muggings, and murder were at an all-time high. High levels of corruption in law enforcement made it appear that the gangsters and drug dealers had control of the city.

On a personal note, there were things about my personality that blocked my path to success. I was stubborn, didn't always finish what I started, sometimes hung out with negative influences, and often rebelled against my parents and teachers.

Despite all of my flaws and the outside forces that surrounded me, I managed to survive, earn my education, and become a mature and successful adult. Many of my friends were not so fortunate; so many went to jail, were killed, and had nervous breakdowns.

The major difference between us was that I had a strong support system of mentors. My family, teachers, and older members of my church took an interest in my life. They taught me to make good decisions, to value myself, and to develop my talents and intelligence. They taught me that my life was special, and that I was here for a purpose.

Growing up in Harlem during those times was like trying to navigate across a battlefield dotted with thousands of hidden landmines or bombs. A wrong move could result in major problems. By teaching me certain principles, all those people that looked out for me gave me a blueprint, almost like a diagram that showed me where the landmines were hidden in addition to where I could find supplies, tools, and shelter. I made more than my fair share of mistakes like any teen, but thanks to the blueprint, I was able to avoid major mistakes that could have destroyed me. Perhaps more of my friends would have been successful too, if they had such a blueprint.

Life as a teenager today is even more difficult these days because the same challenges that confronted my generation are still around today in even greater force. Opportunities to join gangs, sell drugs, and make other crippling decisions are all around you. Broken families, poverty, and violence are close by. It's tough to find work that pays a decent wage, and a college education is becoming more difficult to afford. No, it is not easy being a teenager in America today.

But just because you're young, it doesn't mean you have to give in to challenging circumstances. You can make it around all the traps and live a successful life *if you have the right blueprint*. By "blueprint" I mean the right information, values, attitudes, skills and habits that will help you make good decisions and help you reach your full potential.

This book provides such a blueprint. If you understand and apply the principles and strategies I outline, you are virtually guaranteed to gain respect, success, and power in all the right ways. If you take this information seriously, it can help you make sense of yourself and the world around you.

Don't believe the hype, my young reader. You were not born to be a loser. You are on this Earth for a specific reason. With some guidance and discipline you can discover that reason, develop your talents, and grow into a successful and respected adult.

Your family's background doesn't matter. Your income

level doesn't matter. The neighborhood you live in doesn't matter. Your body type, your attractiveness, your clothing, your popularity, none of these things matter. *What will ultimately make or break you is what you know, what you do, and how you think about yourself and the world around you.*

Get ready to embark upon the greatest journey you will ever take . . . the journey to respect, success and power! How do you get there, you might ask? By developing your **MIND and** your **HABITs, of course!** You will learn the following things in this book:

- The importance of loving yourself
- How to develop self-confidence
- How to prepare yourself *right now* for the future
- How to make good decisions
- How to choose friends
- How to manage your time
- The importance of aiming for excellence
- How to avoid major traps in life
- Thinking like a winner
- How to handle peer pressure

## HOW TO USE THIS BOOK

### HOW THE BOOK IS STRUCTURED

*Truth for Our Youth* contains two parts. Part I - which is the majority of the book - contains 10 chapters, and is written specifically for you and other young people. Part II which contains 5 chapters, was written specifically for your parents, or guardians. You can read Part II also, just as your parents are free to read Part I in addition to the section for them.

I just wanted to make sure that this book had something to offer for teens and parents, because "it takes a village to raise a child." This means your empowerment and success is a team effort. Who better to work with than the people responsible for you? By providing information for both you and your parents, you can work together. So please make sure you have your parents read Part II of the book so they can understand what they can do to assist you in becoming the most powerful teen and adult you can be.

### READ/REVIEW THE BOOK OFTEN

*I wrote this book to change and possibly help save your life.* This book was not written to lay hidden or collect dust on your bookcase. It is a reference book. This means you can and should use it over and over again. I recommend reading the entire book from cover to cover the first time. Take time to complete every activity, and feel free to mark the book in places you find very helpful.

## Do the Activities/Exercises

I include some activities in this book to make you think and to help you develop strategies to improve yourself. Do not skip these activities! Every word and exercise in this book was placed there for a reason. If you skip anything, you might cheat yourself out of important information.

## Review the Big Ideas

Each chapter in Part I of this book ends with a short section called "Big Ideas." The purpose of this section is to summarize and review the most important points of each chapter. Reviewing the "Big Ideas" section after each chapter can help you remember and absorb the information presented.

## DISCUSS THE PRINCIPLES YOU LEARN

After you finish a chapter, discuss the material with your friends and family members. This will promote good conversation, and will help you better remember the principles. By all means, if you enjoy the book and find that it is helpful, recommend it to parents, teachers, and friends!

So, are you ready to learn principles that will make you a positive statistic? Are you ready to show the world what you're made of? What are you waiting for? Let's get ready to fly!

# THE GREATEST LOVE OF ALL

The more you praise and celebrate your life, the more there is in life to praise and celebrate.

Oprah Winfrey

What comes to mind when you hear the word "Love?" Valentine's Day? Marriage? Hugs and kisses? Poetry? These are all forms of romantic love. Love can involve all these things and more. But for the purposes of this chapter, I want you to think of love differently. Love involves service, appreciation, work, sharing, and having a positive image of something or someone.

To begin, you will do a brief activity that will help you identify what things you love and will help you think of why you love them. I've created a list of 10 things and persons many people love. Remember, we're not talking about romantic love. The questions you should ask are: How do they add to your life or help you? What would life be like without these things? Which of these things are you more or less willing to sacrifice or do without? How much time and energy do you put into these things or people?

After you've thought about these things, rank each item. Using numbers 1-10, rank each thing in order of how much you love it. For example, if family is the thing you love most, place a number 1 next to it, and so on until you come to the thing you love least, which you will rank with a number 10. Take your time, and be honest.

| | | | |
|---|---|---|---|
| Country | _____ | Culture/Race | _____ |
| Family | _____ | Boy or Girlfriend | _____ |
| God | _____ | Neighborhood | _____ |
| Pet | _____ | Hobby/Activity | _____ |
| School | _____ | Friends | _____ |

Before we continue, review the list, to make sure you ranked each item as accurately as you could. Remember, there is no right or wrong answer here. No one will grade this. In a short paragraph below, explain why you chose your number one love. Be specific, and use the questions I raised before to answer the question.

I love _____ the most because:

_____

_____

_____

_____

Good! We are going to come back to what you wrote later in the chapter. By then, your answer may change!

You may not have noticed, but I left a very important person off of the list. Here are a few hints: This is one person you wake up with and go to sleep with everyday. You would not exist without this person. Without this person, nothing else really matters to you. And, you will be with this person for the rest of your life, through good and bad, sickness and health, wealth or poverty. If you haven't guessed by now, the important person I'm talking about is you! Isn't it odd that we often forget to mention ourselves when we think about the things we love?

My goal with this chapter is to help you recognize the need to embrace, value, and respect yourself. If you already have a healthy dose of self-love, great! But if you struggle to respect and value yourself, this chapter will really help you. There's no way you can lose here!

From my own experiences growing up, and my experiences as an adult working with youth, I believe that self-love is the greatest love of all. It is the building block of true happiness, respect and success. In fact, your ability to truly love anyone or anything else is built upon the love you have for yourself. Let me go even further. I believe that *young people who have difficulty loving themselves jeopardize their chances to enjoy productive and successful lives in the future.* Notice that I start this book with a chapter on loving yourself. Why? Because if you do not love, respect and appreciate yourself, no other principle in this book will do you any good.

Right now, you might be thinking, "*Of course I love myself, doesn't everyone?*" You'll be surprised to know that everyone does not truly love themselves. Many people say they love themselves, but their actions and attitudes tell another story. True love involves respect, good values, sacrifice, positive attitudes, and healthy choices.

I've developed a checklist below that provides traits of a person with a low level of self-esteem. Read through the checklist and check each item that describes you. Again, be honest. This activity is not designed to embarrass you, but to help you identify the things you must work on. This is the only way you can improve yourself. When you're done, you will have a realistic picture of how much you respect and value yourself. If you feel insecure, and struggle with loving yourself, you may tend to:

- ☐ Adopt a phony identity; try to be something or someone you are not
- ☐ Shy away from people and activities that could help you
- ☐ Bully, make fun of, criticize or gossip about other people
- ☐ Associate with people that don't like you to get attention and fit in
- ☐ Participate in activities (crime, gangs, drug use) that threaten your freedom and safety
- ☐ Refuse to give your all in school or anything else that is positive
- ☐ Eat too much, or too little
- ☐ Become promiscuous (overindulge in risky sexual behavior)
- ☐ Experience serious depression and suicidal thoughts
- ☐ Blame outside people or circumstances when you fail or suffer

If you checked *anything* on this list, you really need

to read this chapter carefully. You might suffer from low levels of self-esteem and self-love. But don't worry. You can and will begin to overcome this if you keep reading!

I'd like to share something with you: talent and intelligence do not guarantee a successful or happy life! You can have all the ability and intelligence in the world and still fail as an adult. The world is full of examples of talented teens that had everything going for them, only to later waste their potential and lead miserable and unfulfilling lives. In addition to making good decisions and thinking for yourself, you must develop a sincere and unwavering love for yourself. You must be comfortable in the skin you're in, or all of your talent and intelligence will amount to nothing!

Your faith in and love of yourself will pull you through the hard times in life, and keep you focused and hopeful despite challenging outside circumstances. Self-love and confidence are like bullet-proof vests that protect you from harm.

On the other hand, once you no longer have hope, you no longer care about the consequences of your actions. You become a feather in the wind, just floating from one situation to the next with no plan or direction for your life. Anything goes and anything is acceptable. People like this are traveling on the road to failure and pain. When you learn to love yourself, you'll no longer drift around; you will begin to steer yourself where you want to go. See the difference?

For those of you that checked any item on the list, I still have good news for you. You don't have to end up miserable or defeated in life. You can change and improve with the correct guidance. History is loaded with examples to prove my point, but let's just look at two case studies.

I want you to read about two people that struggled in their teens, two people that were on the road to failure, but turned their lives around and became great.

### Case Study #1 – Malcolm X

Most people know Malcolm X as the courageous and articulate Black Muslim leader who taught Black people to appreciate their culture, create their own schools and businesses, and to organize and fight for their freedom and empowerment. Many people honor his birthday as an unofficial holiday, and his life was documented in a movie starring the Academy Award winner, Denzel Washington. Hundreds of schools and avenues are named after him, his autobiography is required reading in many college courses, and he even has his own United States Postage stamp!

Read his autobiography however, and you'll find that young Malcolm had plenty of problems. A racist mob killed his father when Malcolm was a young child. His family was poor and often went without proper meals. Malcolm's mother had a nervous breakdown and was shipped off to a psychiatric ward when he was still a child. He and his siblings were separated and sent to different foster homes where they were raised by white families that didn't understand, let alone respect and nurture them.

Despite these circumstances, Malcolm excelled in school, and became his class president in 8$^{th}$ grade. Then one day, his favorite teacher told him that his career goal of being a lawyer was unrealistic for a Black person. "Be a carpenter," he advised him, "You'll never be a lawyer." Hurt and depressed, and facing family struggles, Malcolm dropped out of school in the 8th grade.

The once bright and confident Malcolm slowly began to lose self-esteem and hope as a young adult. He eventually engaged in criminal activities ranging from burglary, to prostitution, drug selling and illegal gambling. He became a drug addict and landed in prison for burglarizing someone's home. Even in jail serving a ten-year sentence, Malcolm behaved so violently that inmates and guards nicknamed him "Satan."

I'm sure that anyone who knew him during that time would predict a terrible future for Malcolm. Years later, he admitted in his autobiography that he hated himself, and that he acted like an animal. He didn't love or value himself, and his actions demonstrated it clearly. It seemed that Malcolm's life was going downhill fast.

But then Malcolm ran into another inmate that introduced him to the religion of Islam as taught by an organization called the Nation of Islam. Among other things, this organization taught Black people to be proud of their rich history, to maintain a healthy diet, and to develop their intelligence and character.

Over time, these teachings had a strong effect on Malcolm. He began to take himself seriously and to develop a sense of purpose. He no longer saw himself as a violent convict and drug addict, but as a strong and proud Black man. He began to study the entire dictionary to increase his vocabulary. He read anything he could get his hands on, and soon became knowledgeable about religion, history, philosophy and politics. He joined the prison debate team and learned to express himself with intelligence and power. He stopped fighting and causing trouble, and eventually was released from prison three years earlier due to good behavior.

A healthy dose of self-love and a change of attitude and habits turned Malcolm's life around. Within a few short years of his release from prison, he grew into a national leader and spokesman. With only an $8^{th}$ grade education, he debated and often defeated national figures with impressive college degrees. Now, approximately 50 years after his death, people are still inspired by his speeches and his vision for Black empowerment.

Around 1980, a young boy in 7th grade was grounded by his mother for the weekend. Bored and restless, he found his father's book of Malcolm X speeches and finished it in a day. The principles in that book changed his life. He idolized Malcolm and committed his life to learning and teaching youth to be proud, strong, and powerful. That young boy was me.

## Case Study #2 - Oprah Winfrey

Oprah Winfrey has too many accomplishments to mention in a book of this size. But here's a few:

- First African American woman to become a billionaire.
- Founder of the largest book club in the world.
- Only the third American woman in history to own her own television production studio.
- Academy Award nominated actress.
- Voted one of the 100 most influential people in

America.

- Host of the most popular and watched television show host in history.
- Winner of more than 40 Emmy Awards. And the list goes on.

But just like Malcolm, Oprah Winfrey experienced a very difficult childhood. She grew up in what we call today a "broken family." Her parents were unmarried and separated teenagers. Her father ran off to join the military at 20, and her mom – who was 18 years old - was a housemaid. Unable to support Oprah, she asked her mother to raise her. Oprah's grandmother raised her until she was six years old, and gave her all the love and support any child could want. With this type of nurturing, Oprah began reading at the age of three, and was considered a "gifted" child.

Her mother came back to get Oprah six years later and raised her until she reached 12 years of age. Those were difficult and painful years for young Oprah. Her cousin raped her when she was 9. Her uncle and family friend molested her. According to Oprah, she began to hate herself. She had frequent fights in school, and became promiscuous and hot-tempered. Talking about those times, Oprah later said that she found herself ugly, confused, and hopeless. Things got so bad that her mother attempted to place her in a youth detention center. When notified that the center had no more room, her mother sent Oprah to live with her father in Tennessee when she was 12.

Loving but strict, her father provided the structure and discipline she desperately needed. Oprah began to excel in school and got into far less trouble.

Oprah still had her share of problems however, and became pregnant at the tender age of 14. Her child later died stillborn. Her father refused to give up on her, reminding her that she was special, loved, and extremely intelligent. He enforced a strict curfew for Oprah, and made her read a book every week. Afterwards, she was required to write a book report on each book she read.

Boosted by a new sense of confidence and self-love, Oprah took her life seriously. At age 19, she became a reporter for a local radio station. She attended Tennessee

State University and won the "Miss Black Nashville" and "Miss Tennessee" pageants. Upon graduation, she got jobs in radio and television, and the rest is history. See how she acted when she didn't value herself? She how her life changed once she did?

Both her story and Malcolm's teach us that nothing, your income level, family background, or even your bad decisions can stop you once you begin to truly love and appreciate yourself. They both had childhoods that may have been more difficult than yours, yet they made their lives count. The love they developed for themselves, along with some help from other people, turned their lives around for the better. The lesson here is that even if you are at a low point now, you can change that if you change the way you think about yourself, and change your negative habits.

**The Difference between Winners and Losers**

I want to let you in on a little secret. No one is born to be successful or a failure. No one is "lucky" or "unlucky." Yet, some people manage to be successful while others don't. This has little to do with their wealth, education, or family background. So how do you explain how one person succeeds while another fails? Attitude is part of the answer. Some people possess a winning attitude and some have a losing attitude. In this section you will learn the difference between the two. Look at the charts on the next two pages.

| Losers | Winners |
|---|---|
| Have a low level of self-confidence; think of themselves in negative ways | Are confident in themselves; have a healthy and positive view of themselves |
| Tend to make excuses; blame other people or outside circumstances for their actions and the consequences of those actions | Take responsibility for their own actions and the consequences of those actions |
| Think that their life is already planned out for them and that they have no say in how it develops; tend to believe that some people are lucky and some are not | Understand that they have the ability –through their attitudes and behavior – to make their life what they want it to be |
| Tend to base their decisions and actions on what "they" say or do; motivated by others | Make decisions and do things based on their own values and goals; are self-motivated |
| Spend most of their time and energy complaining and whining about problems | Spend most of their time and energy analyzing their problems and working on solutions |
| Can rarely tell you what they want to do with their life, because they rarely think about it; have no plan for the future; just drift around | Often think about their future and have a plan for the future, even if it is not complete; make specific moves to get where they want to be |

| | |
|---|---|
| 👎 Feel insecure, threatened by, and resentful of people who may be happier and more successful than themselves; "hate" on other people | 👍 Are secure and confident; feel inspired by people who are more successful than themselves; may even observe such people closely and ask them for advice; congratulate and encourage other people |
| 👎 Very irresponsible with their time; tend to be lazy and to procrastinate; often finish things late, do things at the last minute, and often leave things incomplete | 👍 More likely to use their time wisely; organize their time to complete important tasks; tend to complete things on or ahead of time, and usually finish what they start |
| 👎 Often think their goals are "impossible"; talk themselves out of trying or doing things, thinking it will be a waste of time anyway | 👍 May think of goals as challenging or difficult, but never "impossible"; enter things with the belief that they can accomplish them |
| 👎 Relies on hearsay and gossip; does not take time to seek out reliable and accurate information for themselves; may assume they know it all, or don't want to know any more than they already do about something | 👍 Puts little faith in hearsay or gossip; will investigate and research to get the information they need; sees themselves as a lifelong learner; reads, researches, and asks for advice from reliable sources |

Notice that none of these behaviors are forced on anyone. Losers and winners *choose* to be who they are. Make the choice to be a winner right now. Make a copy of this chart and tape it somewhere in your room where you can see it every day. Train yourself to recognize when you are acting like a winner or loser. Identify the losing traits you possess and slowly begin to eliminate them. The choice is yours to make.

I want you to stop reading for a moment and do an activity. You are going to interview two adults. Afterwards, I will help you analyze the results. I guarantee you that their responses will better help you understand the points in this chapter. You will also see the principles I describe are real.

Try to identify two or three adults that will be comfortable talking to you about themselves. Set a time to speak with each one separately. Explain that you're doing an activity from a book you're reading, and that you'd like to interview them for about 20 or 30 minutes. Assure them that the information they provide will not be shared with anyone. Make sure you do these interviews at times when they are available, not distracted and in a relaxed mood. Have a pen and paper on hand to take notes or use a voice recorder. Ask them the following questions:

1. Do you describe yourself as a successful or unsuccessful adult? Why?

2. Are you satisfied with your life today or disappointed? Why?

3. Think back to when you were in middle school or high school. Name 3 things about yourself that made you proud. Name 3 things that caused you to feel embarrassed.

4. Describe 5 positive qualities about yourself as a teenager. Describe 5 qualities about yourself that you would change if you could go back in time.

5. Describe 5 positive and negative qualities about yourself as an adult.

6. Name 3 decisions you made as a teenager that benefited you in major ways. Name 3 decisions you made during this time that you regret, and explain why.

7. Identify your greatest success or triumph as an adult. What contributed to this success? Identify your greatest failure or defeat as an adult. Who or what contributed to this failure?

After you complete both interviews, analyze the information you gathered. You want to understand the thinking and behavior of each adult. I am pretty sure that you will notice some patterns.

You will probably find that the more happy and successful adults will answer the hard and sensitive questions that others cannot. As you listen to their responses, you'll see that your interviewees exhibit many of the attitudes in the chart I provided. I strongly suggest that you stop here and do the activity before you continue reading.

After completing these interviews, you will see for yourself the difference between a winning and losing attitude. What separates winners and losers has little to do with money, looks, intelligence, or even ability. More often than not, the key difference lies in their attitudes, effort and level of self-discipline. This is great news for you and other teens because it means that anyone can gain respect, success and power over their life!

* * * *

## Strategies to Gain Confidence and Self-Respect

Now you know the importance of loving and

respecting yourself. You've learned how self-hatred and low self-esteem damage your potential and ability to grow. You've read about real people that failed because they didn't respect themselves, and about real people that were able to change their lives for the better once they did. You interviewed people you know personally to discover how their image of themselves affected their lives. In the process, you discovered the difference between a winning and losing personality.

It's time to look at yourself, to increase your own level of self-love, so that you can use the rest of this book effectively. This book is all about you, your growth, and your success.

In talking with young people like yourself, I've developed a list of things they are uncomfortable with or wish they could change about themselves. These things are important because they often affect whether young people like you value themselves or not:

- Attractiveness (face)
- Weight
- Height

- Hair texture/length
- Popularity
- Clothing
- Racial/Ethnic background
- Lack of talents/special abilities

Do any of these things sound familiar? Even adults worry about some of these issues. I've read several self-improvement books. They all discuss the need to love yourself, but many do not provide you with strategies for doing so. I want to share a simple but powerful secret with you, an idea that all successful people understand: *they simply don't spend time worrying about the things they can't control!*

**Strategy 1**

Our first strategy draws from this idea. This activity will help you distinguish between the things you can change and those you must learn to accept. Use the space below to make your own list of the things you don't like or wish you could change about yourself. Feel free to use a sheet of paper if you need more space to write.

*Things I do not like about myself*

1. _____
2. _____
3. _____
4. _____
5. _____

Now draw a line through the items you can't change. For example, if "height" or "ethnicity" is on your list, put a line through them. Since you cannot change them, there's no sense losing any sleep over them. Accept these things, and learn to appreciate them. You cannot love yourself in sections; you must love yourself completely. When you stop worrying about things beyond your control, they will no longer have power over you or cause you unnecessary pain. Learning to accept the things you can't control will also free up the time and energy you need to address the things you **can** change.

One of my favorite sayings is a Chinese proverb which states, *"It is better to light a candle than to curse the darkness."* Now picture this scenario: there you are sitting in complete darkness. Which is a more effective strategy, to complain about the darkness, or light a candle to provide some light? This means you should solve your problem rather than whine about it.

Some of the things you dislike about yourself can be improved in practical ways. Instead of whining about them, create a plan to improve or change them. The items on your list with no line through them represent things you have the power to change. I want you to go back to your list. Look at these things and come up with a way to address them. Here's a brief example of what I mean:

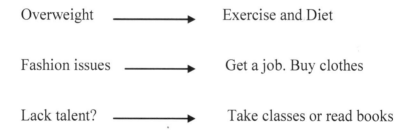

Overweight ⟶ Exercise and Diet

Fashion issues ⟶ Get a job. Buy clothes

Lack talent? ⟶ Take classes or read books

Use the space below to continue on your own, identifying the things you can change and creating a plan to produce the change you want. Again, use a sheet of paper if necessary:

*I don't like:*                    *My Plan:*

_____        _____

_____        _____

_____        _____

_____        _____

This strategy will make you a winner rather than a whiner. Winners don't whine, and whiners don't win. As you focus on the things you can change, you begin to exert control over your life. As you improve yourself in these areas, you will gain more confidence and self-love.

**Strategy 2**

The last strategy helped you to improve or eliminate things about yourself that you don't like. This strategy will help you appreciate the qualities you do like about yourself. My grandmother used to say "Even a broken clock is right two times a day." So no matter how much of a loser you may think you are, there are some things about you that are special.

Always have a balanced and accurate picture of yourself. You possess strengths and challenges. Dr. Martin Luther King Jr. often gave a powerful sermon in which he reminded his audience that no one can excel in everything or be blessed with every good quality. The challenge, he said was that we must identify the qualities or talents we have, develop them, and use them to the best of our ability.

What you lack in one area, you may compensate for in another area. You must learn to be proud of your own special talents or qualities. Identifying what makes you special can protect you against insults from people that want to crush your spirit.

Now I want you to think about yourself and the things that you do like. Use the space below to write down 5 of these things. They can be physical things or qualities of your personality.

- ✓ _____
- ✓ _____
- ✓ _____
- ✓ _____

✓ _____

These are the things that make you feel special and proud. Embrace these things and do what you can to maintain and improve them. Take a sheet of paper and write the headline "What Makes Me Great." Underneath, list the 5 things you just wrote. Post this list in a place where you can see it everyday. When you are tempted to call yourself a loser, when you feel lonely, or when others tease you, remember these good qualities you possess.

Maybe you're in good physical shape, are intelligent or have a good sense of humor. Perhaps you're a good athlete or dancer. Whatever qualities you choose to highlight, remember they are **yours**, and no one can take them away from you.

Use both of these strategies. Over time you will appreciate yourself more, your confidence will grow, and others around you will notice the change. Because you think highly of yourself, others will too.

In other words, self-love is contagious; when you feel good about yourself, others will too! Likewise, if you go around hating on yourself, others will pick up the vibe and treat you similarly. So the next time someone asks you who or what you love the most, I hope you say, "Me," and really **mean** it.

## Big Ideas

- ♥ Self-love is the most important love you can develop
- ♥ If you do not love and appreciate yourself, you are on the slippery slope of unhappiness.
- ♥ Never allow anyone to make you feel unimportant
- ♥ Study the lives of people that struggled at first then changed their lives around; learn from their example
- ♥ Loving yourself involves having a positive attitude and view of yourself and your body
- ♥ Accept the things about yourself you cannot change and refuse to waste time worrying about them
- ♥ Identify the things you don't like about yourself that you can change, and set up a plan to improve those areas

- ♥ Identify the traits you do like about yourself and use this knowledge to protect your self-esteem

- ♥ Use the chart to identify "losing" traits you have; Create a plan and work hard to eliminate them

- ♥ Real love starts on the inside and works outwards; appreciate yourself and others will follow

## PLAY CHESS, NOT CHECKERS

*Again and again, the impossible problem is solved when we see that the problem is only a tough decision waiting to be made*

Robert H. Schuller

Have you ever made a decision that you seriously regretted later? You know, a decision that resulted in upsetting your parents, hurting yourself or someone else, or in a loss of privileges? If so, join the club, because every human being has done the same.

Wouldn't you like to know how to make wise decisions, the types that bring good results? Aren't you tired of staying in trouble while some of your friends seem to just get things right the first time? If you make choices you want to smack yourself for making, or if you ever asked yourself, *"Why did I do that,"* then you're reading the right chapter, my friend!

You are about to learn a process of making decisions that work for you rather than against you. Take heed, and you will make much better decisions – and suffer a lot less – in the future. Also remember that using the approach you're about to learn can also help with controlling and managing your anger and with negative peer pressure.

But before we begin, I have to tell you how I came up with this system. Between 1993-1995, I worked as an In-School Suspension coordinator within a middle school in Syracuse, New York. It was like holding detention during school hours. The goal was to punish students without sending them home, so that they could still receive instruction. Also, my principal was well aware that students suspended out of school often got into even more trouble.

My room had a bathroom and about 15 desks. Students "serving their time" were not allowed to leave the room except in case of a medical emergency. They were even banned from being in the cafeteria, so students brought lunch to them. Talking was not allowed, except to ask questions their assignments. Boring, right? That was exactly the point. If you were deprived of social time and forced to do work all day, you would never do anything to return, right? I say the same thing.

Yet, students did return, time and time again. In-school suspension was successful in keeping these kids off the streets, and they did keep up with their schoolwork. But it didn't change their behavior. Despite the silence and the prison-like atmosphere, they kept coming back to In-School Suspension!

I knew a change was needed, so I broke with school policy and began interacting with the students. My goal was to build a relationship with the students and get to know them. I also wanted to understand and help them understand why they got into trouble so often, and help them to correct their behavior.

What I discovered was that these students had poor decision-making skills. Instead of making rational decisions in their best interests, they allowed emotions and impulsive decisions to get the best of them. So in an effort to teach them how to make better decisions, I did what any responsible adult in my position would do. I listened to their concerns, gave them strategies for making better decisions . . . and taught some of them to play chess!

"Chess? What type of punishment is that," you might ask. I admit my approach was unusual, and it did get me into trouble with the principal at first. She literally pulled out my job description and asked me to find any mention of playing chess! Teachers began to grumble also: *"You mean this guy punishes students by allowing them to play games?"*

I caught heat for that decision, but to everyone's surprise – even mine, I admit – the strategy worked! The same students no longer received in school suspension, and new students that came didn't return. Of course, students kept getting into trouble, so I always had anywhere from 2 to 7 teens to deal with. But it was an improvement from the 10 to 15 youth that used to be there.

To protect myself from getting fired and to prove that the system worked, I developed a short survey to determine if these students improved after being in the suspension room. All the teachers I surveyed said the students were more patient, more relaxed and less likely to cause trouble. But get this... the teachers also said these students actually performed better academically! They were all shocked and very grateful. In fact, some of the very teachers that once criticized me later encouraged our principal to let the chess playing continue.

What the principal and teachers did not understand was that chess is not an ordinary game. Various studies show that chess playing helps you improve critical thinking skills, patience, math ability, concentration, and **decision-making ability**. By 2007, the advantages of chess were so well documented that 30 countries included the game in their elementary school curriculums!

## CHESS VS. CHECKERS

The problem with many teens like yourself is that you

approach life like a game of checkers. What you will soon understand is that life works a lot more like the game of chess. To understand this, you must recognize the difference between the two games.

Checkers is a fast-paced game that is usually over in less than 15 minutes. The pieces all basically move the same, and therefore, your options are very limited. Moves are usually made very quickly and without much thought. Also, the objective of the game is very simple: you win by capturing all of your opponent's pieces.

Chess is completely different from checkers. In chess, there are eight distinct pieces that all move differently and all have different values. Some move

vertically and horizontally, others diagonally, and so on. You can actually have more pieces than your opponent and still lose! Unlike checkers, where the moves are limited, there are over 10,000,000 possible moves you can make after the 7$^{th}$ move! This makes chess a more complex game than checkers.

Chess is a game that requires you to think several moves ahead. In checkers, you usually think about your next move. In chess, the very best players think as much as 20 moves ahead. Now that's some serious thinking! Because chess is so complex, a game could last anywhere from 5 minutes to over an hour depending on the skill level of the players.

Of all the games in existence, chess is most like life because it involves having sound strategy, understanding rules, and making decisions that benefit you in the future.

## A Good Decision Starts With the Right Questions

So how can you think like a chess player even if you never played the game? Simple. A good chess player asks several questions during the course of the game. If you train yourself to ask similar questions before making a decision in life, your decisions are more likely to result in good results. There are some typical questions a chess player must ask herself before making a move.

Every move is offensive (starts action), or defensive

(responds to an action), or a combination of both. A good chess player asks the right questions, comes up with the right answers, and then makes the best moves based on those answers. Everything they do is well-planned and designed to establish a specific result.

In a typical chess game a player might ask themselves dozens or even hundreds of questions, but most are variations of the following.

*Defensive- responding to what someone else did or is trying to do:*

- What is this person trying to do?
- How does this affect me?
- How should I respond?
- Can I afford to lose this piece?

*Offensive – starting an attack; doing something your opponent must respond to:*

- What is my goal in doing this?
- Is there a better move to make?
- How will people respond to my move?

In chess, you have an opponent to deal with. In life, you

may not always have opponents, but maybe situations to respond to, people to deal with, or problems to solve. Let's examine the 7 questions above. We are going to explain them and use them in real life situations.

## *Why did he or she do that?*

You ask this question to understand a person's intentions or their motivation. Based on your answer to this question, you can respond accordingly. Your mother pulls you aside one day and says you must quit the team you're on because it's interfering with your schoolwork. You have a fit because you love being on the team. Before you do something you'll regret later, ask yourself, why did she do that? Is it because she likes making you angry? Does she want to make sure you don't have a life? Listen to her explanation: she says your involvement in the sport is interfering with your schoolwork.

Your mom values you getting a good education so you can be in control of your life as an adult. Although her decision will deprive you of something you love, she's doing it because she has to protect you from yourself. If she allows you to put sports over your education, you might not get promoted to the next grade, or you might miss out on learning some crucial skills and information. Her concern is that you have your priorities all mixed up.

Instead of rebelling against her, why not address her concern? Ask if she will allow you another month to play on the team. If you still fail to pull your grades up, then you will quit the team. But if you can do well in school and play the sport, ask if she'll let you stay on the team. That's an intelligent decision because you demonstrate that you understand your mom's concern and you come up with a fair plan to address her concern.

Your decision shows your mother that you are mature and reasonable. It also shows her that you do value your education. Because you took the time to really understand why your mother did what she did, you can work with her and avoid getting into further trouble.

Your strategy not only meets her concern about school, it gets you what you want . . . to continue playing your favorite sport. Both you and your mother win, and it may increase the level of trust and respect your mother has for you.

On the other hand, let's say you get mad and decide to disobey her orders. When she finds out you dismissed her authority, she will lose trust in you, and may even give you a far worse punishment. Please don't forget that this may also cause your grades to suffer!

## *How does this affect me?*

This is a question about consequences. You want to know what will happen to you as a result of what someone has done or how you respond to it. Your friend calls you up saying they have "beef" or trouble with gang members in his school. He tells you that the gang members threatened him and that he wants to retaliate. He asks you to come with him to confront the other guys.

What could possibly happen to you if you go out with him seeking to hurt somebody? For one, you might get seriously hurt or killed; you might wind up hurting someone else. You might get arrested, imprisoned, and get a criminal record.

Even if you just go with your friend and don't do anything, the gang will see you came there with your friend. They may associate you with your friend. They might see you as their enemy and try to harm you too. You ask yourself, how will this action hurt or help me? You come to your senses and tell your friend that you don't want to be involved. Sure, your friend will question your loyalty to them, and may not want to be your friend anymore, but isn't that better than possibly getting arrested, hurt or killed over something that doesn't concern you?

Let's say you're in an after school tutoring program. You signed up because you're failing math and social studies. But your boyfriend has other plans. He tries to persuade you to skip the tutoring and come over to his house. He explains that no one will be there and you two could hang out by yourselves.

Ask yourself what can possibly happen if you go with your boyfriend. You will get to spend time alone with him, and may have a good time. But if you skip tutoring, you miss out on information that will help you pass your classes. In other words, you may have a good time if you go, but your grades and school performance might be threatened. Not to mention that if your or his parents find out, they will lose trust in you, and might even ban you from seeing him again! Will hanging out with him in this instance hurt or help you? Just asking this question may prevent you from making a bad decision.

## *How should I respond?*

Your English teacher returns your essay, full of red marks, criticisms and a failing grade. You are upset because you worked hard on that essay, and thought it was your best effort. The low grade you received concerns you because it might affect your general grade in the class. Moreover, it hurts your pride because you believe you're a good writer. How should you respond? You have a number of options. You can:

1. Get mad, accuse your teacher of picking on you, and bring your dad to school to argue with the teacher.
2. Just accept the grade
3. Tell your teacher that you want another opportunity to do the essay.

The first approach would not be wise. It would embarrass your father when he found out that you lied and that you possibly deserved the grade you received. The second approach of doing nothing about it isn't ideal because it robs you of your power to choose and solve problems. The third approach is a good one since it demonstrates maturity and a willingness to work hard. Also, it might actually lead to a positive grade change!

Many times it's not about what happens to you, but how you choose to respond that makes the difference. Always choose to respond in ways that solve your problems and prevent additional ones.

### <u>Can I afford to lose this piece?</u>

This is a question of priorities or values. You ask this to determine if something you have is worth keeping or losing. Let's say you're walking in your neighborhood one day and a group of thugs attempt to take your smart phone. You notice that one of them has a knife or gun. Your pride tells you to fight for your property. But first ask yourself: can I afford to lose that phone? If they take it, can I get another one? The answer of course, is "Yes." But what can happen if you choose to fight for your phone? You might get injured or even killed. Is your phone worth dying over? Is it more important than your health and safety?

By asking these questions you realize that you can replace the phone, but not your life. Unless you're a superhero or martial arts expert, you will not be able to beat all the guys by yourself. Even if you're carrying a weapon, you don't want to hurt or kill someone over a three or four hundred-dollar smart phone. The best decision in this case would be to give them your phone. This may seem corny or weak to you, but just look at the news and observe how many young people are killed over a jacket, jewelry, or cell phone. These things are important to you and might be expensive, but you can exist without them. You cannot exist without your life. Always remember to prioritize things in your life.

## *What is my goal? What am I trying to accomplish?*

This is a question of objectives. You ask yourself this question to be clear about why you're about to do something. Asking this question will ensure that your actions help you to achieve your goal.

Imagine that you have a job for the summer. You took the job because you want to buy some clothes without having to depend on your parents. Although you don't make much money, you are able to finally purchase a few things for yourself. But you begin to miss out on other things your friends are doing. You wish you didn't have to get up so early for work. You'd rather sleep late and have the entire day to yourself. As a result, you begin entertaining the idea of quitting your job.

Before you make that decision, remind yourself why you're working in the first place. You have a goal of improving your wardrobe and becoming more independent, right? If you quit the job you will have no source of income and therefore no way to accomplish your goal. Sure, you can get another job, but that might take weeks or months. You realize that if you quit the job, you may have more time on your hands, but you will not meet your goal.

As a result, you decide to sacrifice your time in

exchange for buying your own clothes. This is a good decision because it helps you. Quitting the job would be a poor decision because it would make your objective more difficult to reach.

## *Is there a better move for me to make?*

This is a question of being efficient. There is usually more than one way to reach your goal. A wise person will compare different strategies and use the one that saves the most time and energy and ends with the best consequence. You get in an ugly argument with a friend who has done something to violate or disrespect you. Your instinct is to bust him in the mouth. That is one of your options, but certainly not the best one. Responding to disrespect with more disrespect will only make your problems worse. "Fighting fire with fire" is a popular saying, but when you think about it, the statement makes no sense. Your goal is to put the fire out; therefore you should fight fire with water. In this case, you might conclude this person is not really your friend at all. Maybe you should limit your contact with this person. They can't violate you if you're not around, right? Besides, hitting your friend might get you into trouble with school, the police, or the friend's family members. In addition, both of you might be enemies forever.

## How will people respond to my move?

This is a question of perception and consequences. You ask this question to determine how other people will react to you. I'm not suggesting that you live your life based entirely upon what others think. However whenever you're in public, it's like you are on a stage. You do not exist in the world by yourself. You must interact with other people, and you must learn to be aware of how people perceive you.

People constantly watch you and form opinions about you. They will deal with you based on how they perceive you. Other people's opinions can hurt or help you later on, so be aware of how you contribute to their perceptions of you.

Never forget the law of cause and effect. Your actions and words create reactions. Before you do something, you should give some thought to how people will react. Only very immature people go through life doing things without thinking of how people will perceive or respond to them. Then some of these same people wonder why people avoid them, treat them badly, or don't trust them.

Let's say you are invited to a party at a friend's house. At some point, you become thirsty but when you look around you notice that all the sodas are gone. You figure that your friend's parents must have some juice or soda in the fridge. You walk into the kitchen preparing to open your friend's fridge and get a drink.

First ask yourself how your friend and his or her parents will respond to this. They might be offended if you go into their fridge without permission. The party hosts may perceive you as a rude and inconsiderate person with no home training. As a result, they might not invite you back into their home. Your friend's parents may even get upset with their child for bringing you into their home in the first place.

In other words, your action may cause people to resent you. I would! Wouldn't it be better for you to just ask the parents for something to drink? Also, shouldn't you get the parents' permission to go into their refrigerator?

Time for another activity! Think back and reflect on 2 choices you made that resulted in bad consequences. Use the chart below to identify 2 bad decisions you made in the past. Indicate the effect of each decision.

| Bad Decision | Effect of the decision |
|---|---|
| 1. | |
| 2. | |

Now come up with a better choice for each decision and indicate the likely result of each decision.

| Better Decision | Likely effect of the decision |
|---|---|
| 1. | |
| 2. | |

In conclusion, please remember that life is a game of chess, not checkers. Your life is an accumulation of the decisions you make. Show me an unhappy and unsuccessful person, and I'll show you a person that repeatedly makes poor decisions. I guarantee that if you ask yourself the questions we discussed, you will get into the habit of making decisions that lead to good results.

## Big Ideas

- Making good decisions is a skill and process that anyone can learn

- Life is like a game of chess; it involves strategy and thinking ahead

- Decisions can be measured by the results or consequences they create

- Hasty decisions usually result in bad consequences

- Good decisions begin by asking yourself the right questions

Agyei Tyehimba

## SOCIAL ETIQUETTE: DON'T LEAVE HOME WITHOUT IT

*Whoever you are, wherever you are, and whatever you do, you will always be considered wrong if you are rude.*

Maurice Barring

Did you ever become frustrated or upset when a parent asked you to wear a different type of clothing, commanded you to lower your voice in public, or questioned a certain hairstyle you wore?

If so, you are like just about every other teen. During teenage years, you are stronger, smarter, and can do more than you could as a child. You yearn to be independent, express yourself, and make your own decisions, and you often resent when adults question your choices, right? I'm sure you often wish you were an adult so you could do what you want, when you want, and in the manner you want.

No one said being a teen would be easy. In fact, it's often difficult to juggle schoolwork, chores, AND all of your parent's and the world's expectations of you. One of your biggest challenges during your teen years will be to balance your need to express yourself with the need to do so responsibly. This chapter will discuss this and help you to understand the tricky and complicated world of "social etiquette."

Etiquette is a code of behavior that sets expectations for how to conduct yourself in public. What makes this tricky is that this code of behavior is largely unwritten. Although some community groups establish classes (usually for young girls) etiquette is usually taught (or not taught) in households. In time, some of these rules or expectations change.

Also, you do not have to follow these unwritten rules. However, since society expects you to follow them, people who choose not to or who are ignorant of these rules often experience negative outcomes. My goal is to spare you some unnecessary suffering and confusion by making sure you are aware of basic social etiquette.

As is the case with anything else in this book, you can completely ignore my advice. But if you do, *I promise that you will suffer and strain relationships with those around you.*

There are several forms of etiquette. There is work etiquette, business etiquette, dating etiquette, travel etiquette, and so on. This chapter will discuss three basic types of social etiquette that I believe are relevant to young people: personal hygiene and sanitation, clothing and fashion, and cell phone etiquette.

## PERSONAL HYGIENE

Have you ever spoken to someone with horrible-smelling breath so hot and sour-smelling that you suspected they could gargle with peanut butter? Maybe you've been on a public bus or train and nearly fainted when a passenger raised their arm? Or perhaps you know someone in school that everyone avoids except for flies? These people might be nice, but their failure to be clean turns everyone off.

As a teenager, you are expected to practice personal hygiene. This includes brushing your teeth, ensuring your breath is pleasant, washing your body and clothes, and using deodorant. You should do these things first and foremost because doing so protects you from sickness and disease.

Socially speaking, you observe good hygiene because no one wants to be around someone who doesn't. Unclean people attract loneliness, gossip and people that resent them. Your parents and the Internet are good sources to determine how to observe good hygiene. I won't go into that here. But I do want you to understand the importance of doing so, and what happens if you don't.

You must also have sanitary practices which govern what you do when you cough, sneeze, burp yarn, or pass gas in public (you can stop laughing now). Simply put, no one wants or should have to breathe in unwelcomed germs from your body.

There are few things more impolite than inappropriately sneezing or coughing in public. When you do not cover sneezes and coughs, you potentially make other people sick. And when people see you do this, they generally view you as impolite and inconsiderate. You can avoid all of this simply by bending your arm toward your face and coughing or sneezing into the space between your bicep and forearm. And if you must blow your nose, please do so with a tissue and then discard the tissue into a garbage can when you're done.

Burping and passing gas are normal bodily functions. But this doesn't mean you can't do these things without practicing etiquette. When you burp, it is considered polite to turn away from people, cover your mouth and say "excuse me." Similarly, you should either go to the bathroom or remove yourself from other people before passing gas. But if you are unable to do this and cannot hold it, you should say "excuse me." Failing to do this will definitely lose you hundreds of cool points and make you look "uncivilized" and inconsiderate (this goes for young men and young ladies).

**CLOTHING AND FASHION**

As a teen, I'm sure you want to wear clothes and have a style that expresses who you are. This is perfectly normal. However, you will need to express yourself responsibly and in ways that do not embarrass yourself or your family. Lady Gaga may choose to wear a dress made of beef, because she wants to generate media attention and sell albums, but this is probably not a good idea for you.

Let's face it. The primary purpose of clothing is to protect our bodies from the elements and to cover body parts considered private and personal. But in our society, clothing is also considered a form of art we call "fashion." So we also wear clothes to make personal statements and develop a sense of style.

Some young boys currently wear pants way below their waist and down to their thighs. This means they are walking around with their behinds out (a style that originated in jail where inmates are not allowed to wear belts). This also means such boys cannot run freely if they needed to, because their pants restrict their leg movement.

I also notice that some young ladies wear skirts that are quite short, plunging necklines that expose their breasts, overly-tight jeans and an abundance of false eyelashes, hair weave, and makeup. Again, you want to express yourself and that is fine.

But consider this point: the way you clothe your body and present yourself to the world, says things about you to those looking at you. While you cannot please everyone and shouldn't ever try to, you also must realize that with rights come responsibilities. You have the right to express yourself. But you also have a responsibility to do so in a manner that brings honor to your family and that encourages people to treat you with respect.

When you are out and about, your clothing is like a

costume that represents a character in a movie or play. What character do you want to project to the world? One that is immature, silly, and possibly promiscuous? Or one worthy of respect and positive attention?

I recognize that young people have popular clothing styles, and that how you decide to dress is ultimately a choice for you and your parents to make. *Choose wisely!* Here are a few points you should consider when choosing what to wear in public:

- Your clothes should be comfortable and you should feel comfortable wearing them. If you can barely breathe or walk without constantly adjusting your clothes, maybe you should consider wearing something else.

- Your clothes should be appropriate for where you are going or what you are doing. A wedding, church service, sporting event, graduation, all call for a certain type of formal or informal dress code.

- Teens of color (for example Blacks and Latinos) suffer greatly from unfair stereotypes like being "thugs," and "sluts." With this in mind, give some thought to what messages your clothing sends about you to the world. How are your fashion choices likely perceived by other people? Does your clothing encourage positive or negative attention?

- At this stage of your life, when you should be preparing for adulthood, most of your energy and thought should not go into your hair or clothing anyway. Focus on being clean, neat and appropriate in your dress. But spend more time and energy making sure you are developing your intelligence, skills, and character.

**CELL PHONE ETIQUETTE**

Cell phones did not exist when I was a teenager. We had to make calls from home or from a public payphone in a store or in the street. Now that cell phones are common, there is a need for a few rules to govern how we conduct ourselves when using them in public. Again with all rights come responsibilities. Also, your rights should not interfere with the rights of other people.

You have the right to use your phone in public settings, but others have the right to travel on public transportation, or shop in a store without having to endure loud and inappropriate phone conversations.

Other people also have the right to enjoy a movie, play, museum, or library without hearing your phone ringtone blasting music. With this in mind, please observe the following:

- Smart phones have microphones in them that amplify your voice. There is no need to yell; Please lower your voice when speaking in public, whether you're on the phone or not.

- Private conversations are called that for a reason; such conversations are personal, not social. You don't know who is listening to your conversation, and you don't want to put yourself or anyone else in an embarrassing situation. Therefore, refrain from discussing very private things in public.

- Put your smart phone ringer on silent or vibrate in restaurants, theaters, church or the library.

- Choose a ringtone that is not vulgar, inappropriate or embarrassing. Also, don't have it set to play very loud.

- Refrain from texting or accepting non-emergency calls when in the company of people. This is rude.

- The speakerphone function is there to help you have hands free conversations. It is helpful when you are grooming yourself or in the bathroom for example. However, other people don't want to hear you screaming at your phone. Also, you should notify the caller that you've put him or her on speakerphone. They may not want other people to hear their remarks.

## **Big Ideas**

- Social Etiquette consists of unwritten but important rules of conduct

- Using social etiquette helps to distinguish you as a person with good manners and consideration for other people. This will open many doors of opportunity to you.

- The failure to implement social etiquette, especially in very common areas like personal hygiene, clothing/fashion, and using smart phones, will lead people to think badly of you and treat you in a less-than-respectful manner

- Society will hold you to the rules of social etiquette whether you know these rules or not. Ignorance of the law does not excuse you or protect you from the consequences of "breaking" the law.

- How you speak, dress, and exist in public reflects on you and your family. Let your behavior bring honor and not shame to yourself or those responsible for you.

# MESSAGE FOR BLACK YOUTH AROUND THE WORLD

*Each generation must, out of relative obscurity, discover its mission, fulfill or betray it.*

Frantz Fanon

This message is for all youth composing the African Diaspora. "Diaspora" is a term referring to the scattering of people from their original homeland to other places throughout the world. While African people live on almost every part of the Earth, large populations of the Diaspora lives in parts of Asia, North, South and Central America, the Caribbean Islands (like Cuba, Haiti, and the Dominican Republic), and the islands of the Pacific Ocean. The number of people that make up this Diaspora numbers more than 200,000,000 people around the world. These people originally were scattered to other places from Africa. This occurred either willingly (through migration) or against their will (through slavery).

## A brief history lesson

Imagine that you are home alone and you hear sounds outside your door leading you to believe that someone is trying to break into your apartment. You might be scared at first, but then you wisely call your city's emergency number (usually 911).

The operator begins talking to you and asks a few questions. While you attempt to explain the emergency the operator interrupts you and likely asks two questions: "What is your name and address?" This questions deals with who you are and where you are from. Similarly, a well-developed person should know their own name and address or in other words, take pride in his or her culture and ethnicity.

Overwhelming scientific evidence proves that the original people of ancient Africa (prior to European contact) created the foundations of art, law, medicine, spirituality, music, math and science which through migration and contact with others, spread throughout the world. Thus Africa is considered by many to be the "cradle of civilization."

Early non-African historians - notably the Greek historian Herodotus, and Muslim historian Leo Africanus – wrote favorably of ancient African societies, noting how scholarly and advanced they were.

Beginning in the 1400's and increasing in the 1800's, European countries explored and invaded different parts of Africa. They were excited to find huge amounts of fertile soil, trees, diamonds, gold, platinum, and other things they needed to manufacture machines, produce energy, and develop their societies.

By the 16th century, the transatlantic slave trade was underway, dragging millions of Africans from their native land and dispersing them throughout the Caribbean islands, South and North America.

How did this happen? African societal rivalries and Europeans' advanced weapons along with certain religious ideas spread by priests laid the foundation of Africa's continuous mistreatment for centuries thereafter.

Throughout the 1800s, the race to own African territory created disputes among different European nations, all of whom saw African materials and labor as ways to enrich their countries. So in 1884, 13 European nations met in Berlin, Germany to decide what nations owned which parts of Africa. The primary countries that colonized African territories were Britain, France, Belgium, Portugal, Italy, Germany and Spain.

It is important for you to understand that the enslavement and colonization of Africa contributed to the tremendous wealth of European nations and the United

States today. For this reason, some people believe the U.S. and other nations owe members of the African Diaspora some form of repayment or "reparations" to compensate for all that was historically stolen from our ancestors.

> **DID YOU KNOW?**
>
> - Ancient Egypt is one of the world's oldest and longest-lasting civilizations.
>
> - Africa has the largest percentage of precious metals (gold, cobalt, and

Africa's original role as the educational/spiritual center of the world thus gave way to its role as the chief source of cheap raw materials, mineral resources and labor for European industrial growth. The false concepts of White superiority and Black inferiority (white supremacy and racism) developed as European nations sought to justify their greed and brutality toward African people and others.

In a complete reversal of history, Europeans began referring to African people as "primitive and "uncivilized." These developments changed the course of world history.

Centuries of mistreatment, discrimination and unjust laws help to explain why members of the African Diaspora are now among the world's and disadvantaged people wherever we exist on this planet.

**African Independence**

Every human being wants to be free. No group of people enjoys mistreatment or enslavement. After WWII many African nations participated in the African Independence Movement. One by one, former colonized nations fought and won their freedom from the European nations that colonized them. African nations were now free to run their own affairs (though in many cases former colonial powers still manipulated African nations from behind the scenes).

Sadly, some of the African nations that won their independence became dictatorships. A dictatorship is a corrupt and dishonest form of government in which one person (called a "dictator") has ALL of the power. A dictator steals a nation's wealth for him or herself, lives in huge mansions, and rides in luxury cars and planes while most of the citizens live in extreme poverty.

Usually the dictator remains in power for their entire life, so there are no elections. Because the dictator does not welcome any criticism of their corrupt leadership newspapers or television networks that are not government owned are banned. The government does whatever the dictator wants, and whoever has the courage to complain or protest is quickly imprisoned, tortured and even killed!

The countries that colonized Africa were run by white people. The dictators that ran Africa after winning independence were Black. Both killed, stole money and land, and treated citizens badly. The lesson you should get from this segment of history is that regardless of one's race or where one comes from, we can find fairness and cruelty or greed and corruption in ALL types of people.

## The Present

It is vital that you understand this history in order to properly understand the present. Today, though most of us are not literally enslaved, many people of the African Diaspora find ourselves living in conditions of poverty, injustice and oppression.

In America for example, after hard-fought victories against enslavement and segregation and the election of our first Black President, African Americans still have a higher rate of infant mortality, poverty, and incarceration than other Americans. Also we, like people of color in other nations, still suffer from propaganda teaching us that we are ugly, unintelligent, naturally violent, lazy and hopeless.

In summary, Africans and their descendants were made to believe that we are not capable, encouraged to shrink away from taking our rightful place in the world, and led to believe we lack humanity and compassion. Far too often our own behavior demonstrates that some of us believe and behave according to these mistruths. Consider some of the negative behavior and attitudes that *some* of us have adopted:

- No respect for learning
- Accepting overcrowded, filthy and disease-ridden living conditions as normal or "good"
- Embracing a criminal lifestyle and boasting about incarceration
- Disrespect for elders
- Willingness or desire to inflict harm upon members of our own community
- High instances of suicide, homicide, and severe depression
- Believing that other groups of people are smarter, more attractive or "better" than we are.

**Message to Youth**

I'm sure you can see how such beliefs and practices and the oppression that caused them, threaten the well-being of our communities and our future. Given this, I'm calling for you, the youth of the African Diaspora, to reclaim your greatness, honor your ancestors and take hold of your future in the following areas and ways:

## Develop Pan-African Consciousness

The legacy of racism and our forced dispersal all over the world caused us to not only to lose sight of our own value, but to look upon our Diasporan family in negative ways.

Some of us developed prejudices and hatred toward Africans, South and Central Americans, African-Americans, and our people in the Caribbean. This occurs every time you make fun of someone with a different accent, different clothing, or a different language than yourself.

You must educate yourselves to recognize and accept the humanity of all people, which includes people of color. The world is composed primarily of Black or Brown people. Unifying around our common experiences and forming economic and political bases of power will prove most beneficial for all of us in the future. This of course, does not mean that you should be cruel or hateful toward people who are not part of our Diaspora. But you should not be hateful and hostile to your distant relatives around the world either. It is sad and shameful to see Blacks, Asians, and Latinos express resentment for and even discriminate against each other.

Because members of the African Diaspora speak different languages, come from different countries and have embraced different religious and cultural practices, it may seem like we have little in common. Just remember that whether you are Black, Latino or Asian, and regardless of what language you speak, music you like, or food you eat, *we are family*. We were just separated and scattered throughout the world. This is also true whether you are Christian, Muslim, Buddhist or atheist (don't believe in God).

## Health

Without good health, little else matters. People of color die prematurely at rates that are much higher than other people. In addition to having a healthy diet heavy on fruits, grains, and vegetables and light on animal products, You MUST exercise regularly, to build and maintain a healthy heart and other muscles.

Don't forget your mental health also. You must find healthy ways to release stress in your life and get proper medical attention when you need it. This naturally means you should avoid drugs (including Meth, cocaine, heroin, Xstasy and marijuana) that damage your body and mental health. Immature and dangerous forms of "fun" now will cause pain later.

**Learning/Self-Development**

As a young person, your life should include preparation for adulthood in addition to fun and recreation. Many countries make basic education mandatory for this reason. Being a capable worker or business owner in the future requires you to have certain skills like reading, mathematics or science.

Responsible citizenship involves certain responsibilities. It is difficult to be a responsible citizen if you can or do not: 1. Read and understand newspapers, books, laws and important documents of your country; 2. Know basic geography in order to locate and learn about other places in the world 3. Have strong writing skills so you can write editorials in local newspapers 3. Develop public speaking and critical thinking ability to educate other people, protest injustice, debate ideas and policies, or run for local/national political office in your country if you so choose.

In addition to these forms of education, you will also need to develop good character in order to be a fair-minded, compassionate, and responsible adult.

Then there are also non-academic skills you must learn to function effectively in society. Some of these – but not all – you will learn in school. Some of these skills might include:

- Cleaning your household
- Defending yourself
- Prioritizing issues
- Budgeting money
- Learning other languages
- Solving problems
- Organizing people
- Conflict mediation
- Understanding economics

- Managing time
- Logic and Debate
- Critical Thinking
- Effective communication
- Farming
- Hygiene and grooming
- Cooking well-balanced, delicious and nutritious meals
- Creating a business
- Swimming
- Anger management

**Politics**

I'm not referring to formal politics involving campaigns and elections (although that is important) but to identifying problems in your community or nation and working with others to solve them in constructive ways. The world is forever in need of capable, dedicated and informed individuals to lead organizations, create schools and businesses, and overcome poverty, illness, and injustice.

There is plenty of opportunity for you to become involved in leadership. For example, you can become a doctor, lawyer, businessperson, engineer, scientist, historian, teacher, civic and union leader and the list goes on.

Every nation and society no matter how small or impoverished has produced such leaders and organizers. Yours has too, and you should consider continuing that tradition. I would strongly suggest learning about your nation's leaders throughout history (along with those in other parts of the world).

## Healthy Thinking

You are no good to yourself or anyone else if your thoughts and actions are negative and self-defeating. Nor will you be successful if you don't believe in yourself or if you are plagued by envy, vanity, arrogance, and pessimism.

## Conclusion

I've given you much to think about here. My hope is that you will take these words/ideas as seriously as they were intended. Regardless of your place of birth, language, gender, level of education or family income, you are capable of improving yourself, your village or city, and of changing the world for the better.

Refuse to believe the lies that you are nothing, have nothing, and can be nothing! These lies keep us divided and powerless! Stand up and take your rightful place in the world! Learn about the world around you and prepare yourself to play an important role in it. Young people like yourself can and do make a difference with their lives.

I've provided a very basic set of ideas here. The challenge is or you to improve upon and implement them. My generation and those before it have done much to secure AND jeopardize the future of this planet. I call upon you to improve it because I believe in you!

## Big Ideas

- Part of being powerful and successful is knowing who you are and where you come from. This means identifying and being proud of your history, culture and heritage. This also means you should be aware of mistakes, defeats and bad historical memories so you do not repeat them.

- The continent of Africa is the birthplace of humanity. Despite attempts throughout history to mistreat and make Africa seem backwards or uncivilized, its heritage includes great contributions to civilization and monumental achievements. At the same time, you must be balanced. Africa, like all other places, was and is not perfect, and African people are not "better" than anyone else.

- The descendants of Africa, who are located throughout the world and other people of color, have a responsibility to know and be proud of our history and the struggle and sacrifice of our ancestors. You must know your "name and address" in order to move forward with confidence and power in life.

- Members of the African Diaspora, in addition to all other human beings, have a responsibility to educate and empower ourselves. So many people sacrificed so that you life could be better than theirs. Enjoy your life, have fun, but make sure you do your part to make this world a better place for everyone.

## INVEST IN YOURSELF

*Education is our passport to the future, for tomorrow belongs to those who prepare for it today.*

Malcolm X

Your childhood and adolescent years should be fun. But whether you know it or not, these years play a huge part in what your adult life will be. In addition to having fun, it is wise for you to begin developing the skills and information you will need to be a successful and happy adult.

In the United States of America, elementary and middle school education is compulsory. This means that all children are required by law to attend school from first grade to high school. For some children, attending school from Monday to Friday is a real chore. You may not understand the big deal about showing up, paying attention, completing homework, studying, or doing well on tests. As far as you're concerned, you are not interested in some of your classes, feel like some of the teachers are picking on you, and can't understand how **any** of this affects your life in the future.

I understand how you feel because I felt the same way as a student sometimes. What I'm about to share with you is simple yet complicated at the same time, so pay close attention. The purpose of school (from the government's point of view) is to teach you certain habits like being on time, having good attendance, obeying people in positions of authority and following rules. Attending school also is supposed to make sure all citizens have certain basic skills to enable them to be good workers: speaking, writing, problem-solving, etc.

Many of the public schools in our neighborhoods don't have the money or technology to compete with wealthier schools. Sometimes the teachers don't seem to understand or care about you, and are challenged when it comes to making courses interesting and relevant.

What you need to understand is that education in America – especially for young people of color - has several roles. I just mentioned the public agenda of education. But there is a hidden or ulterior agenda for educating young people. By high school graduation, a student has received 12 years of important academic coursework, but you also receive 12 years of social conditioning or programming that is designed to shape and influence how you think and act.

The curriculums you must learn in American history for example are designed to make you honor and admire certain types of "heroes" while keeping you clueless about non-white people and women that contributed to this country or who fought to defend our humanity. You are sometimes encouraged to be patriotic toward American ideals and values, and not to criticize them. You are taught to be obedient and to respect authority even when the authority is unjust. You are also given perspectives of events, individuals and policies that are sometimes inaccurate or imbalanced.

Remember that in some cases, the people that develop school curriculums, create school policies, (and schools themselves) may not understand Black and Brown people, or may have negative assumptions about us (we're violent, intimidating, reckless, can't pay attention, don't want to learn, or we're on the road to prison or gang life).

I've taught in schools where white school leaders and deans have implemented systems of discipline that are overwhelmingly cruel and demeaning to students of color. In one case, I actually resigned because I refused to treat beautiful and talented Black and Brown children like dangerous criminals!

I'm sad to inform you that because of racism, budgetary issues, misplaced priorities, and overcrowding in urban areas, there are simply not enough excellent public schools in this country at the present time. Charter schools have become popular in the United States because they promise to provide safety, discipline and excellent education.

But even some of these schools have few Black or Latino faculty members and some operate more like prisons than places of learning. Nevertheless, even the worse schools still offer very basic information and skills which can help you become an informed and prepared individual.

Reading and writing well, clearly expressing yourself in conversation, knowing how to study, concentrate, debate and being able to do basic math are skills you must have as an empowered adult.

So despite all the problems with public education in America, you can still learn a great deal if you apply yourself and take your future seriously. Some concerned educators, philanthropists, parents and activists (me included) are working to create curriculums and schools that are warm, fun, and safe places for learning.

In the meantime however, **YOU** must invest in yourself and do so regardless of your skin color, gender, living conditions or household composition.

Some of you reading this book are going through difficult times. Your father might have abandoned you. Maybe your mom is in prison, or you live in a foster home or shelter. Sometimes your lights are cut off or you don't eat regularly because your parents struggle to pay the bills. You might wear old clothes or be teased because you speak another language or come from another country. Other students might bully you because of your religion, hair, complexion, poverty or because you are attracted to people of the same gender as yourself. But none of these situations give you an excuse to give up on yourself.

In fact, these conditions give you even more incentive to invest in yourself and learn all you can so that you can change those situations in the near future! This world chews up and spits out the weak, timid, and unprepared. To make it in this world, you will need to be strong internally (character) and externally (skills and preparation).

So many young people invest great time, money and energy in looking good, being popular and "fitting in." I strongly suggest you make the most of these years by investing time and energy into being intelligent, accomplished, skilled, and of good character. Why? Because the quality of your life, your community and this society in the future depends on the work you do **now** to prepare yourself properly.

I'd like to give you a scenario to emphasize the last point. Let's say you and some friends go to a nice restaurant. The waiter approaches and gives everyone a menu. You notice that your friends seem very satisfied with the dishes in their menus, so you decide to open yours and take a look. To your surprise, you review the entire menu and find that only one item is listed . . . French fries!

Puzzled, you call the waiter over and ask for a complete menu. In a sarcastic tone, he tells you that "*the menu you have is the one you deserve.*" He goes on to say that you can only order that one item on the menu!

How would you feel about this? Most likely, you would feel left out and confused. You might even feel angry as you watch your friends debating which of the delicious dishes they will order while you sit there with only one item to select. Either you will order French fries, or eat nothing at all. Quite a dilemma, isn't it?

If you can understand that situation, then maybe you'll understand this: when you fail to educate and improve yourself, you create a very limited menu.

In this case, when I say "menu," I'm talking about an assortment of options or choices. A limited menu of education and skills leaves you with very limited life options. Unlike a person with a solid education and a well-rounded set of skills, you are locked into certain choices. This situation is similar to travelling on a dead-end street.

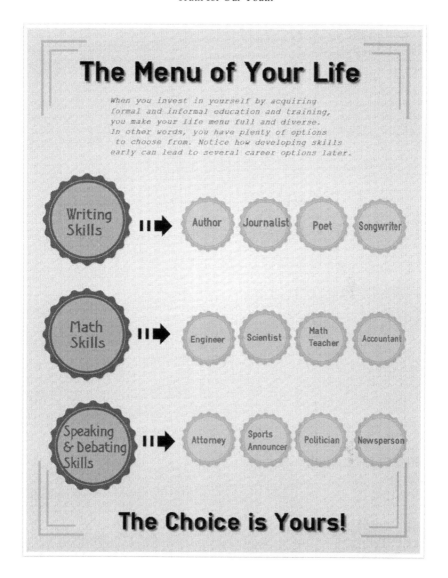

Well-meaning parents and other adults often pressure their children to attend school and get good grades, but don't clearly explain importance of education. Put simply, a good education is designed to provide you with a full and diverse life menu.

You should not acquire education for the purpose of bragging about the diploma or degrees you have. We should not develop skills and knowledge simply to make tons of money, or to be someone's boss. The real value of education is that it prepares you to do several different things, have several options, and it equips you to solve problems and empower your community.

## Formal vs. Informal Education

We should begin by understanding that education takes two basic forms: formal and informal. Formal education refers to the learning that takes place in school. Formal education typically has the following qualities:

- It occurs in a classroom setting

- Most of your information is provided to you by an instructor
- Your progress and performance is measured with exams
- You graduate or are promoted based on your performance (grades, test scores, and attendance for example)

- You are responsible for learning specific skills and ideas which are established by outside people and agencies
- You receive a diploma, degree, or certificate upon completing the requirements

In the United States, you are not required to complete high school and college, though doing so will give you a wider choice of career options as an adult.

Many students your age wish they didn't have to attend school. After all, sometimes school can be a nuisance, right? The demanding teachers, the boring subjects you have no interest in, getting teased by other students, and waking up early can really annoy you at times. Maybe you don't like the notion of being *required* to attend school. When you look at school in these ways, it can seem like more of a chore you do reluctantly.

I'll never forget the day my former fifth-grade student said she would eliminate mandatory education if she were elected President of the United States! What she didn't understand was that such a move would absolutely cripple the country.

Imagine for a moment, a nation where children are not required to attend school. Within ten years, we would have few competent attorneys, bankers, engineers, doctors, scientists, teachers or several other types of professionals. Many citizens would not be able to read or write, do basic math, or run organizations and businesses. Poverty might increase, along with bad health, ignorance and disorder. Our society might be on the brink of ruin!

> **DID YOU KNOW?**
>
> - 4 out of every 5 American millionaires have a college degree.
>
> - College graduates make about 84% more in salary in their lifetime than people with just high school diplomas.

My little fifth-grade student didn't realize all of this, because she wasn't thinking about the future. She didn't understand that all the skills, ideas, and habits she acquired from attending school would benefit her and others once she grew older. Education does have some immediate benefits, but most are long-term! Formal education prepares us to be leaders, workers and problem-solvers later on.

**Informal Education**

We do not learn all we need to know in school settings, however. Our personal experiences, conversations with people, observations, and individual research also provide us with important information. This independent type of learning is called *informal education*, and it's just as important as what we learn in school.

Informal education can take place almost anywhere, but we see strong examples of it in the home, church, and in our interactions with other people. Unlike formal education, you, rather than an expert or instructor, are the guide. There are several ways you can informally educate yourself. Typical ways include:

- Reading books, newspapers and magazines on your own
- Interviewing people
- Surfing the Internet
- Listening to or viewing radio shows, television shows and documentaries

- Attending workshops, sermons or seminars
- Receiving ongoing mentorship from an older experienced person
- Making careful observations of your life experiences

Informal education explains how some people become successful without the benefit of much formal schooling.

Sean "P Diddy" Combs dropped out of Howard University to pursue his dream of becoming a music mogul. Now he manages a clothing line, music label, and other businesses, making his net worth more than $300 million dollars.

Richard Branson, the founder and owner of Virgin Records and Virgin Airlines, did not finish high school. Henry Ford, didn't complete the 8$^{th}$ grade, but went on to create the Ford Motor Company, making him the world's richest man in his day.

How do we explain these success stories? They may not have acquired much formal education, but they managed to educate and empower themselves through experiences, working with people, and their own independent study and research. Never again let anyone or anything get in the way of you investing in yourself.

Remember this motto: "Life is more fulfilling when you invest in yourself properly, but miserable and depressing when you prepare yourself sloppily."

The big idea here is that however you do it –informally formally, or a combination of both – you must take time to develop your skills, knowledge, habits and attitudes. As the United Negro College Fund motto states, "A Mind is a Terrible Thing to Waste." So too is your life.

Don't waste your mind or your life. Determine what your interests are, research the skills and experience needed, then create a plan to develop those skills and experiences. What are you waiting for? Time waits for no one, so get busy!

## BIG IDEAS

- You have a responsibility to invest in yourself through formal and/or informal education.

- Successful people are life-long learners

- 💡 The primary focus of educating and investing in yourself is not just to get a job or develop a career, but to increase your options in life and to develop leadership ability and good character.

- 💡 Self-investment is a serious endeavor and you must work hard and aim for excellence. You get out of it what you put into it. No one should have to "force" you to take your schoolwork or any other training seriously.

## MANAGING PEER PRESSURE

*One who always walks in another's tracks leaves no footprints of their own.*

*Proverb*

A common situation many teens face is peer pressure. Wikipedia defines this as "influence that a peer group, observers or individual exerts that encourages others to change their attitudes, values, or behaviors to conform to group norms." Simply put, peer pressure occurs when your friends and associates "pressure" you to think and act as they deem fit.

Peer pressure has been blamed for many negative teen behaviors including risky (and premature) sexual practices, gang activity, alcohol and drug use, skipping school, bullying, and even rape and sexual assault. I can personally relate to this because I remember well growing up in Harlem and facing peer pressure myself. I regularly encountered pressure to use/sell marijuana and other drugs, fight, have sex, use profanity and a number of other things.

> **DID YOU KNOW?**
>
> - *41% of all teens are pressured to be mean to others*
>
> - *23% teen girls are pressured to have sex*
>
> - *44% of all teens are pressured to lie, steal, or cheat*

Peer pressure among youth (and adults) is common and very influential. Therefore I will not waste time trying to dismiss or sugar-coat this problem. What I will do is provide you with a way of understanding it, and using it to your advantage. In some ways, your ability to understand and manage this pressure can determine your level of happiness and success years later.

Let's begin by understanding the idea of "pressure." Pressure is basically a force applied to an object or person. Did you know that your body deals with extreme amounts of pressure every day? According to scientists, Earth's atmosphere exerts about 14.5 pounds on every square inch of your body. This equates to having about one ton or 2000 total pounds of pressure on our bodies, which is the weight of a small car!

You're probably wondering why your body isn't completely crushed by all of this pressure, aren't you? The answer is scientific. And if you understand this, you will understand how you can resist negative *peer* pressure in your life. There are two reasons your body isn't crushed by all the pressure exerted on it:

1. This pressure exerts itself in all directions, pushing down on you, at your sides, and up from the ground

all at the same time, so it balances out.

2. The air in your lungs and the fluids and bones in your body push back with almost the exact same pressure outwards, balancing out the pressure imposed on you from the outside.

In other words, our bodies have developed the internal strength to counteract the tremendous outside pressure exerted on us. If our bodies did not have this inside pressure, our organs would be crushed and we would die. In fact, when our bodies are exposed to different atmospheres we have to make adjustments to survive. For example, airplanes travel about 30,000 miles over the Earth. At that height, the air pressure is much lighter than it is on ground level. Normally, this difference between the atmospheric pressure and the pressure in our bodies would cause us to get dizzy and lose consciousness at such heights.

To counter this, airplanes are pressurized inside to equal the pressure exerted on them from outside. Also, oxygen masks are provided to passengers to account for the lack of oxygen that we can breathe at great heights. Similarly, we must use oxygen tanks and special outfits to deep-sea dive because at deep levels, water exerts enormous pressure on our body.

So how does all of this scientific talk relate to peer pressure? In the same way that our bodies are internally strong enough to prevent being crushed by outside pressure, and in the same way that we must adjust ourselves to different environments in order to survive, we must do the same in our daily interactions with peers or... we won't survive the journey of life!

People who are confident and think for themselves, develop the inner strength to counteract negative peer pressure from their peers. So the question is: how do you develop the inner power to prevent negative peer pressure from robbing you of success? Here are a few ideas:

- Meditate: Take 30 minutes each day (15 in the morning and 15 prior to bedtime). In the morning, find a quiet place where you're alone. Sit in a chair with your hands folded on your lap. Close your eyes and breathe slowly. Remind yourself of how important, strong and powerful you are. Visualize yourself having a good day and tell yourself that you will make good decisions and that you will not follow behind others. At bedtime, do the same only this time, review the highs and lows of your day. Give thanks for what went well. Take note of what didn't and vow to make the next day better. You are not speaking aloud but in your mind.

- Read the biographies or autobiographies of people you deeply respect and admire. Note how these people had to take charge of their own lives and make their own decisions. See the attitudes and qualities these people have in common.

- Think of a relative that gives you good advice and who demonstrates they want the best for you. When people try to make decisions for you, or lead you into taking certain actions, imagine that the relative is right there. Picture their face and voice. Ask yourself, "What would he or she say about this?"

- Use the chess player's method of decision-making discussed in chapter 3.

- Always think about cause and effect. Every choice or action has a result or consequence. Ask yourself, "What is likely to happen if I follow behind my friends?" Is this a situation I want for myself?" It helps if you think about specific people you know or see everyday that have done the things your friends are encouraging you to do. Concerning sex, think about all the people your age that you see walking around with baby carriages. Think about how you hear young mothers and fathers complaining about finding a babysitter, paying for diapers, food, and daycare, or not being able to do the things they want to do. Concerning drug selling, think about someone you know or know of who sells drugs. Then think about how they went to jail or have people constantly looking to harm or rob them. Concerning stealing, think about a thief you know and how they do jail time, get beat up when caught, or have a bad reputation.

Smart people don't have to personally experience things to know they are not good. They can observe what happens to other people or follow wise advice.

When I was a little boy my father would take me on walks through our Harlem neighborhood. At that time – the 1970s – it was common to see several drug addicts out in public. He would point such people out to me and tell me to closely observe them. He always asked me, "Do you want to be like that when you grow up?" I observed such people and noticed their bodies and clothes were filthy. They couldn't stand up straight. They had ugly bruises and cuts all over their faces. They couldn't speak well. Often, they begged people walking by for money, and I noticed that people didn't respect them.

These walks with my father had a strong influence on me. I made up my mind as a child NEVER to become a drug addict! Later, as a teenager and then adult, these images never left me and when peers used drugs like Cocaine and Heroin, I never joined them.

All human beings make errors in judgment and you are no different. However, you can develop the ability to resist peer pressure simply by knowing when to say "no," and by trusting your intuition, that little voice inside that gives you advice throughout your life.

Negative peer pressure will usually make you feel uncomfortable. You will get the feeling that an individual or group is trying to persuade you to do something that goes against your values, will harm yourself or others, or that will produce a negative result. When you feel this way, do not be afraid to say "No thanks." Never be afraid to leave that environment. Sometimes your peers will tease you, call you names or try to make you feel guilty. "You're a momma's boy," "You're wack," "I thought you were my friend," "Everybody does this," are some of the things you'll hear.

At times, they will make fun of you so much that you will feel sad, angry, embarrassed, or like you don't belong. But if you stay strong on the inside and ignore them the day will come when some of these same people will admire you and even ask for your help in various ways. Your goal is to live a happy and successful life. If doing that means losing some friends or getting teased, that's a fair price to pay, don't you think?

To deal with peer pressure (you definitely will and probably have already), here are some useful tips:

- Work on loving and respecting yourself
- Involve yourself in positive activities with positive people
- Develop a set of goals you want to reach
- Always think about the consequences of your actions
- Follow your intuition

- Consult parents and positive adults for advice
- Say "No thanks," and walk away
- Suggest another activity
- Avoid peers that do dangerous or inappropriate things
- Get people on your side by explaining why a certain activity is not a good idea
- Identify things you will and will not do

All teens like you want to belong, be accepted, and have friends. And all teens will face peer pressure. Follow the tips we discussed, build up your inner strength, and always think about the consequences of your actions. Your parents or guardians will not always be around to help you. This is something you must do for yourself, and often in their absence. I have faith that you can and will resist negative peer pressure now and in the future. Now go out and prove me right!

## **BIG IDEAS**

- Negative peer pressure is a normal part of teenaged life. You cannot escape it, but you can learn how to deal with it effectively.

- Your friends have enormous influence over you. When they attempt to pressure you to do things that will harm you, get you in trouble, or violate your principles, you must have the internal strength to resist such pressure.

- Anticipate peer pressure and develop techniques like the ones I suggested to deal with it. Remember that what you do or don't do is always your choice. Choose wisely and don't worry about being corny or getting teased. You have the right and responsibility to look out for yourself.

## AVOID THE TRAPS!

*An ounce of prevention is worth a pound of cure.*
Benjamin Franklin

I really wish I could tell you that life will be easy and smooth for you. But if I did, I'd be lying. The truth is, being an adolescent or young adult is not easy. No matter how talented, intelligent, or confident you are, no matter how strong your family is, you will face certain traps in life. Knowledge of these traps and how they can damage you can help you avoid them if you are wise enough to listen.

There are a number of traps that await young people. If you can avoid these traps, your life journey will be much smoother and far more productive, though your life will never be perfect or without problems regardless of what you do. In the last chapter, we discussed the importance of resisting peer pressure. Now you will learn about some of the specific things peers might pressure you to do.

## DRUGS

According to the Office of Adolescent Health, at least half of all teens abuse an illicit drug at least once by their senior year in high school. The most popular substances used by teens are alcohol, cigarettes and marijuana, but other substances include "Crystal Meth," prescription medications, and even glue. Young people also use dangerous drugs like cocaine, heroin and "ecstasy" as well.

Drug and alcohol use are very dangerous. Addictions often develop which are very difficult to overcome. The harsher immediate effects include brain damage, imprisonment and even death.

But there are also other disastrous effects of using drugs: You damage relationships with your family and friends; Your schoolwork suffers; You become more prone to accidents and injuries; Your ability to make good decisions suffers; You are more likely to steal, lie, and be dishonest in an effort to get drugs; You waste precious time and money; Your physical and sometimes mental health declines. Did you ever have a dream in which you were scared, nervous, confused, acting silly and didn't understand what was going on around you? That is similar to how you feel when you're high on drugs.

## WHY TEENS USE DRUGS

If using drugs often leads to addiction, shame, disrespect, poor grades, bad hygiene, arrest, and violence, why do so many people use them? Good question! Young people use drugs for a variety of reasons: to become more outgoing and acceptable to friends, to overcome fear, or to escape feelings of stress and anxiety. You will sometimes have these feelings; they are a natural part of life.

Drugs might temporarily make you feel strong, happy, confident, and peaceful but that's in the beginning. Continued use of drugs almost always leads to bad decisions and even worse situations.

What you must learn to do is develop ways of feeling good that are healthy and productive. Review the following table for some ideas of how to respond to negative emotions in a healthy way.

| ANXIETY | -Meditate or pray<br>-Play relaxing music<br>-Exercise<br>-Breathe deeply and slowly<br>-Take a walk |
|---|---|
| DEPRESSION | -Avoid people that complain/whine<br>-Play upbeat music<br>-Visit school social worker<br>-Write poetry/Do art<br>-Watch comedy shows |
| ANGER | -Exercise<br>-Play relaxing music<br>- Breathe deeply<br>-Sit or lie down<br>-Think about positive things |

## INCARCERATION

Although certain studies suggest that youth incarceration in America is declining, too many adolescents and young adults are subject to arrest and imprisonment. The United States incarcerates more youth than any country in the world. Of these, Black and Latino youth are imprisoned at far greater rates than other youth.

I'd be willing to bet that you like to be independent and make your own decisions, right? If you are like many other young people, you probably don't like to:

- Be told when to go to sleep
- Be told how to use your free time
- Be told what you can and cannot eat
- Wear clothing you don't like
- Have a curfew imposed by your parents
- Have your parents tell you when and what you can watch on television
- Have your parents choose your friends

Well guess what? If you don't like having your parents make all of these choices for you, you will absolutely HATE jail or prison! Once you are in prison, many of your rights  are taken away and other people make choices about your life. The warden and corrections officers (prison guards) have the authority to regulate what and when you eat, when and how long you can exercise, what you can wear, where you can go, when you wake up and go to sleep, etc.

In addition, prison officials will determine when or if you can watch television, when you can take a shower and for how long, and who can visit you. Doesn't sound like fun, does it? That's because it isn't!

But how can anyone treat you like this in America? What happened to your rights as a U.S. citizen? Prisons can regulate just about every area of your life (whether you like it or not) because of the 13th Amendment to the United States Constitution, the highest law in our country.

The 13th Amendment outlaws enslaving any U.S. citizen or making them do work against their will. This Amendment was created to end the enslavement of African (Black) people in the United States of America during the 19th century. But the Amendment mentions one exception to the no-slavery rule....people convicted of crime CAN be forced to do work against their will. Section 1 of the Amendment states:

*Neither slavery nor involuntary servitude, **except as a punishment for crime whereof the party shall have been duly convicted**, shall exist within the United States, or any place subject to their jurisdiction.*

Perhaps this is why prisoners are often referred to as "state property."

Imprisoned youth face a number of unfortunate conditions: Most youth correctional facilities are overcrowded and understaffed. These environments also generate tremendous violence like stabbings, theft, fights, and worse. This environment is not one that creates harmony and peace. Many times, inmates are almost forced to become violent just to protect themselves from the violence surrounding them.

But the problems don't stop there. Having a criminal record often makes your attempts to get a job very challenging. It can also damage your reputation and even prevent you from voting in presidential elections. In short, getting "locked up" puts you in a ditch that is difficult to exit. I strongly urge you not to involve yourself in situations that lead to your arrest and/or imprisonment. Once in prison, you become a modern-day slave. Heed the warning!!

## GANGS

Gangs are a serious problem in the United States. They exist in our neighborhoods, schools and within prisons, and they account for large amounts of violence and crime. According to the Federal Bureau of Investigation, there are about 33,000 gangs in the U.S. and they account for almost 50% of the violent crimes in some sections of the country.

Gangs are so dangerous because they involve so many harmful things including: drugs, violence, imprisonment, and dropping out of school.

Do you know a friend or peer that is in a gang? Are you

aware of all the difficulties and dangers that come with gang life? Do you even know how a person joins a gang, and the things they are expected to participate in once they do?

## WHY YOUTH JOIN GANGS

Most young people want to belong, be accepted, and feel independent and powerful. I'm sure you do. Have you ever wanted to feel protected, have money, respect from your peers, and the ability to do what you want to do when you want to do it? People join gangs for all of these reasons and more. Gang members have their own rules and they often go against the rules of society. Young people often admire and are attracted to the rebellious and independent nature of gangs.

Gangs provide protection for their members; gangs swiftly punish anyone who dares attack or disrespect a gang member, and such revenge usually involves violence and intimidation.

For youth that have been abandoned by parents, kicked out of school, or ignored by peers in their neighborhood, gangs represent a family to which they can belong. Regardless of how you look, dress, or how popular you are, a gang will welcome you and make you feel at home . . . as long as you follow their rules and do what members are expected to do.

---

**DID YOU KNOW?**

- Gang members are 60 times more likely to be killed than non-gang members.

- 40% of gang members are under the age of 18.

- The majority of serious gang members eventually drop out of school.

---

How do you join a gang? What do gangs expect you to do? Usually you join a gang by volunteering to commit a crime, or by being "jumped" in. This means that several members of the gang assault you at the same time. If you can withstand the attack, you are initiated into the gang.

You can also be "sexed" in. In this case, girls get

initiated by having sex with several boys in the gang. But the most typical way of joining a gang is to commit a crime: steal something, assault someone, etc.

Gangs establish these forms of initiation to make sure they can trust you, to determine how "tough" you are, and to teach you the expectations and responsibilities of gang membership.

Now let me ask you a question: Would you trust a friend that beat you up, forced you to have sex, or made you do something illegal to prove your friendship? Probably not. And if you wouldn't do these things for a friend, you shouldn't do them for ANY organization that claims to support and love you.

If you want to *triple your chances of being assaulted, killed, or thrown in jail,* then joining a gang is the thing to do. If you want to be healthy, safe, and positive, you need to stay away from gangs.

## TEEN PREGNANCY

Preachers and parents usually approach this topic from a moral point of view. They suggest that sexual activity outside of marriage is fornication, which is a sin. I am no religious authority and I think it is more effective to give you the practical reasons why having children as a teen is not in your best interest.

Rates of teenage pregnancy in the United States have been declining for the past 20 years. However, the reality of "children having children" still exists. Children are precious, and having them is necessary to prevent the human species from becoming extinct. However, most teenagers lack the emotional maturity, finances, and skills to be excellent parents. Please don't confuse my point. I'm not calling you or your peers stupid; I'm calling you *unprepared* for this important task.

## WHAT DOES IT TAKE TO BE A GOOD PARENT?

Being a parent is probably one of the most fulfilling but difficult non-paid jobs in the world. Just review the following list of important things a good parent must do and ask yourself if you're ready to assume the responsibility of becoming a parent.

*Good Parents Must:*
- Cook
- Clean
- Buy food and clothes
- Pay rent
- Wash and clothe their children
- Teach children good values/provide good advice
- Make sure their children attend school
- Prepare their children to be successful adults
- Discipline their children
- Make sure their children are safe
- Provide medical care
- Involve children in educational and fun activities

Quite a few responsibilities, right? You thought doing your household chores was tough? Just imagine being a parent! And unlike most other jobs that have a definite start and end time, parents must be on call *all day everyday* from the day their child is born until at least 18 years of age when a child legally becomes an adult. Even after a child turns 18 years of age, a good parent is still on the job (providing money, buying clothes, giving advice, paying college tuition, etc.).

Also, once you become a parent, *your life is no longer your own.* Much of your time, money, energy and thoughts go to raising, protecting, clothing, feeding, and preparing your child.

For example, you are invited to a party, but in order to go you have to arrange for a babysitter; You want to buy a new cell phone or pair of sneakers but before you do that, you have to make sure your child has clothes and food; You have a part-time job that doesn't pay much money; with the little money you have, you must buy diapers, toys, food and clothes.

Here's a realistic scenario for you: You've just finished a hard day of work. You're exhausted, hungry and grumpy and you can't wait to grab some food and go to sleep. But you can't; you still have to pick up your infant up from daycare, feed her, wash her, and play with her. You finally finish all of those responsibilities and you're ready to relax and watch your favorite television show. But right after you grab the remote control, your baby starts crying loudly. You try holding her in your arms, singing, changing her diaper, but she keeps crying, forcing you to miss eating, sleeping or watching TV until several hours later. The child's needs come before yours.

By now you have probably noted that being a parent involves good amounts of money, time, attention, maturity, and patience. You will admit that these are not things the average teen has in great supply. This is no negative judgment of you or your peers. It is simply the truth. Most 13-19 year-olds have not accumulated enough life experience, education, skills, emotional maturity, money or patience to be good parents.

## Problems Associated with Teen Pregnancy

You may already have a child or have friends your age that do. I want you to understand that all children are precious, and no child is "illegitimate," "a mistake" or a "problem." I am not judging teens with children.

However, I would be lying to you if I didn't explain that *having a child as a teenager seriously complicates and changes your life.* So please, don't be defensive or get upset. Just try to really understand the problems associated with teen pregnancy.

> **DID YOU KNOW?**
>
> - Only 1 out of 3 teenage moms earns a high school diploma
>
> - Only 5% of teen dads stay with the mother of their child after the child is born.
>
> - Babies born to teenage moms are more likely to be underweight, premature and sickly.

If it seems like I'm focusing mostly on teen moms and not teen dads, that's because only about **5%** of teen dads stay involved in the young lady's life after she gets pregnant! So even though parenting is just as much a young man's responsibility as it is a young woman's, in most cases, young ladies will unfortunately do the major share of parenting if they become pregnant.

## Dropping out of School

In chapter 6, we discussed the importance of investing in yourself. When you make the decision to drop out of school prior to earning your high school diploma, you seriously damage this investment and make your adult life much more challenging and difficult.

**The disadvantages of dropping out**

1. You will earn about $375,000 less over your lifetime than a student that earns a diploma.

2. Since colleges and universities require a high school diploma or General Equivalency Diploma for admission, not completing your high school education means you won't have access to "Higher education." Since a person with a college degree earns approximately 1 million dollars over their lifetime, you also lose out on a huge amount of income if you drop out before or during high school. Since many good jobs require a Bachelor's degree, your career options become more limited without one.

3. Due to less than ideal jobs and therefore poor job benefits like good medical insurance, people that do

not complete their high school education are more likely to experience poor medical treatment and poor health than high school graduates.

## ABUSIVE RELATIONSHIPS

Relationships -either romantic, familial, or just friendly - are the cornerstones of life. They make life worth living, right? But relationships involving intimidation, violence, distrust and control have no place in your life.

These types of relationships are abusive, and abusive relationships have a way of destroying your self-confidence, and making you depressed or angry much of the time. This is no way for you to live, no matter how "cute" you believe your boyfriend or girlfriend to be.

Our discussion on this subject is brief. No one you date has the right to abuse or mistreat you. Abuse in relationships can take different forms:

**Verbal abuse** occurs when the person you date constantly yells at you, curses you out, name-calls or speaks in ways that embarrass or humiliate you.

**Sexual abuse** occurs when the person you date forces you to kiss, have sex or do something sexual to or with them or others against your will.

**Physical abuse** involves getting beaten, assaulted, or physically attacked in any way.

**Emotional abuse** is often more complicated than the other forms of abuse. This is because many normal and decent people participate in this form of abuse, without even knowing it sometimes. Examples of emotional abuse may include someone making you feel guilty, treating you like they are your parent, making you feel inferior or that you need them, giving you the silent treatment for long periods of time, making you feel indebted to them, etc.

The subject of abusive relationships is tricky. No one is perfect and everyone at times does or says things they regret due to anger. Even the best relationships involve arguments and immature behavior sometimes, even in romantic relationships between older adults.

What I'm trying to say is that even nice people that really care about you will sometimes do things that upset you and that are not appropriate. But there is a big difference between a decent person that occasionally makes mistakes, and a truly abusive person.

Generally speaking, an abusive person *consistently* makes you feel:

- Like your opinions and feelings are invalid
- Like you are stupid or incompetent
- Intimidated, unsafe and uncomfortable
- Worthless
- Angry and resentful
- Depressed
- Incomplete
- Like you need him/her in your life
- Like you cannot think for yourself
- Like you need his/her permission to do things
- Like everything you do or think is wrong
- Physically or emotionally damaged

- Overwhelmingly guilty for not spending more time with him or her.

In addition, you should be aware of the qualities of an abusive person. He or she may:

- **Be insanely jealous.** Abusers don't want you speaking to other people and often accuse you of flirting or cheating on them. While they will try to say their jealousy is a sign of love, it is really a sign of immaturity and insecurity.

- **Isolate you from other people.** Abusers are very uncomfortable when you socialize with anyone besides them. He or she may attempt to prevent you from seeing other friends or going anywhere without them.

- **Have a history of abuse toward former mates.** If you inquire about a person that is abusive, you will often find that he or she was abusive to other people in past relationships.

- **Become overly-aggressive during arguments.** An abuser will frequently hit, shove, or grab you during arguments. They may try to prevent you from leaving by physically getting in your way or blocking the door. They might throw things at you or purposely damage things that belong to you.

- **Threaten you with violence.** This needs no explanation.

- **Never take responsibility for his or her actions.** An abusive person rarely recognizes the role he or she plays in bad things that happens. In his or her mind, everything that happens to them is someone else's fault.

If you believe a person you're seeing is abusive, I would suggest sharing this information with your parents/guardians and school counselor to receive further advice. Just remember this: people that truly love you and value you do not generally hit, hurt, embarrass, or make you feel unsafe, or unworthy. YOU and your parents should be the only ones exerting control over you, certainly not someone you call your boyfriend or girlfriend.

## TIPS FOR MANAGING YOUR TIME

*Don't be fooled by the calendar. There are only as many days in the year as you make good use of. One person only gets a week's value out of a year while another gets a full year's value out of a week.*

*Charles Richards*

Sometimes life just isn't fair is it? Some people are very wealthy and powerful. They can get what they want, when they want it. People like this can purchase the best cell phones, tablets, video game systems, clothes, sneakers, or other items.

People considered very attractive have doors of opportunity opened for them that others sometimes don't. Highly intelligent or talented people also have certain doors in life open to them, as do celebrities.

People of color (Blacks, Latinos, Asians, Native Americans) and women on the other hand, often face unfair discrimination because of our race or color.

But there is good news. TIME is life's great equalizer. Regardless of wealth, neighborhood, race, or attractiveness, ALL people have exactly 60 seconds in a minute, 60 minutes in an hour and 24 hours in a day.

Much of life is unfair, but we all have equal amounts of time! Mastering a skill, saving money, breaking a bad habit, developing new skills, losing weight or building muscle, all require TIME. If you can manage and organize your time, you can master just about ANYTHING! This chapter will show you just *how* to do that.

## Managing time means organizing it effectively

If you are regularly late to school, your part-time job, or anything else, you are probably not organizing your time effectively. If you always miss important deadlines, or find yourself rushing to get things done, you are not properly organizing your time. If you often forget to do chores or other tasks, you are not organizing your time effectively.

### Tools of Time Management

So how do you organize your time? Well, you can start by using certain time management tools that you might take for granted: a watch, calendar, daily planner, and "Things to do" list.

A *Watch or clock* is the foundation of all time management. It is almost impossible to organize your time or stick to a schedule if you don't know what time it is at any given moment.

A *calendar* – like a clock – also allows you to measure time. But instead of measuring hours and minutes, a calendar measures days, weeks, and months. You can also use a calendar to keep track of important events or tasks.

A *daily planner* is a form of calendar that provides you with a small and large view of each month, a daily view of each day in every month, and spaces to write important notes or reminders.

A "*things to do list*" is a simple list you can create yourself, in which you write down all of the important tasks you need to accomplish each day.

When I was a teenager, we literally had to purchase or use these tools separately. As I got older, we could store all of this information on a big, bulky desktop computer. But these days, you are fortunate to have a form of technology that makes time management simple. It's called a *smart phone or tablet.*

Which of your smart phone's features do you use the most or think are the most helpful? The camera? The Internet? Texting? Video chat? Apps like Instagram or Facebook? I enjoy some of these features as well. But your smart phone has features that can really help you organize your time.

For example, your Smartphone or tablet has a built-in clock, calendar (which is also a daily planner), and memo or things to do feature. All the basic tools you need to manage your time effectively exist within *one device you use all of the time!*

I will not spend any time explaining how to use these features, because your user manual will explain it all probably better than I can. However, you should know that you can put important events or "things to do" into your phone's calendar (complete with location and time info) and even set your phone to vibrate or send you an alert when an event is approaching so you don't miss it. You can also use the alarm feature to make sure you wake up or begin a project on time. You never have to be late, forget a task, or miss a deadline again!

Having access to all of these great tools means **nothing** however, if you don't first understand WHY you need to manage your time, or HOW to manage it.

## WHY YOU NEED TO MANAGE YOUR TIME

As I suggested earlier, managing your time can prevent you from being late, forgetting important events or tasks, and developing skills important to your career and life as an adult later.

There are additional benefits to managing your time which include: wasting less time, being more productive, becoming a more reliable person, experiencing less stress, and having more time to enjoy yourself. There is no way around it – the need to manage time effectively never goes away. Time management will make you a higher-performing student, a more productive and well-respected

> **DID YOU KNOW?**
>
> The average American teenager spends almost 8 hours a day watching television, listening to music, playing video games, talking on the phone, texting, using social networks and/or surfing the Internet? 8 hours is equal to a full day of work!

worker/business owner. and a happier and more fulfilled person.

In 2011 the entertainer Justin Timberlake starred in a science fiction movie called *"In Time"* which really demonstrated the importance of time in our lives. The movie is set in the year 2169. Paper money and metal coins don't exist. Time is the only currency used, and with enough time you can purchase whatever you want and live in the best neighborhoods.

Scientists found a way to put a digital clock inside of everyone's forearm. At birth, everyone's arm clock has 1 year. Once a person reaches 25 years old, they stop aging. At that point, the clock counts backwards from 25 years down to 0. Once your clock reaches 0 (meaning you've run out of time) you die instantly as if someone unplugged you from an outlet! Workers get paid with time, and people purchase things with time. You can give or take time from someone by holding your forearms next to each other. Poor people live life day-to-day, in constant panic, rushing everywhere, because they have so little time available. Wealthy people live pampered relaxed lives without worries because they have thousands or even millions of years on their clocks.

This is a science fiction movie so it's not real. However it shows you just how valuable time is and how time affects your quality of life.

## How do you manage your time?

Good time management is a habit and not one that develops overnight. It is also a process that involves a few steps. The very first thing you need to do is to determine and distinguish between the things you need to do versus the things you want to do. As you know, all of these things use up time, and in order to have the time to address all of these things effectively, you must organize and *prioritize* your time. Prioritizing time means you determine what tasks are most and least important and you make sure such tasks receive the appropriate time or attention.

The things you **need to do** include things like household chores, bathing, brushing your teeth and other forms of personal hygiene, class work, homework, and basic necessities like sleeping and eating.

The things you **want to do** are self-explanatory. These things include the things you truly enjoy, like recreational time with your friends, athletic activities, and other hobbies or interests.

The first thing you must do is realize that like money, time is "spent' and must be budgeted wisely to make the most of it. How do you budget time? You can start by taking one day of your week and keeping track of the things you do each day, and how much time you spend doing these things.

Remember that each day you have 24 hours, no more and no less. Use the following chart below to begin. If you do the same things for the same amount of time every day, you only have to do one chart. But if for example, your weekends are scheduled differently, or certain days of the week are busier than others, you must do separate charts for those days.

## Monday

| Activity | # of Hours |
|---|---|
| School | _____ |
| Team practice | _____ |
| Homework | _____ |
| Chores | _____ |
| Sleep | _____ |
| Video games | _____ |
| Television | _____ |
| Bathing | _____ |
| Exercise | _____ |
| Total Hours | _____ |

When you finish this, you'll want to pay attention to which activities get most of your time. You want to make sure that the most important activities get more of your time each day. And yes, the total hours cannot exceed 24.

Just doing this alone will greatly help you to prioritize your activities. When you do this, you can make sure the most important and empowering things in your life receive the majority of your time and attention. The more time you put into developing yourself and prioritizing your activities, the greater your chances of success later.

If you find that too much of your time goes to unimportant things like watching television, playing video games, or posting things on Facebook or Instagram, you can begin reducing the time you spend on such things and allocate more time to important activities.

Now that you've identified your priorities and least important activities, and made changes to the amount of time you've assigned them, there is one more thing you should do. You now have to develop a *schedule* for each day. This means you will use the calendar on your phone to identify the things you do each day, along with the time you do each activity. For example, you might have a schedule that looks something like this:

6:30-7:30 am: Wake up, shower, get dressed, eat breakfast
7:31-8:00am: Travel to school
8:01am-3:00pm: School day

3:01-5:00pm: Homework at library

5:15pm-6:00pm: Snack, phone or Internet

6:10pm-:700pm: Dinner

7:10pm-8:00pm: Evening chores

8:10pm- 9:30pm: Family time

9:30pm-10:00pm: Shower, iron tomorrow's clothes

10:00pm: Bedtime

This is just a sample schedule. Yours will look different based on your family's habits, and your activities. As you schedule your day, remember to be flexible. Unexpected things will always pop up when you least expect and you will have to adjust your schedule. There's nothing wrong with that. If you go off schedule and miss a few tasks, it's alright.

I will assure you that budgeting your time, defining your priorities, and scheduling your day are habits that will help you master your time.

## BIG IDEAS

- Time is one of the few resources that everyone has

in equal amounts.

- Time is similar to money in that you can spend it, waste it or budget it. Unlike money however, once time is gone, *you can never recover it*.

- How you use your time now usually determines the quality of life you'll lead in the future.

- In order to make the best use of time, you must identify how you spend it, how you waste it and how you should schedule it. To do this you should use important tools like a clock, calendar, a things to do list and daily planner. Most of these tools exist on a smart phone.

- You must prioritize your time. This means that you should spend more time doing the activities that are most important and beneficial to you.

# HOW TO CHOOSE FRIENDS WISELY

*Choose your friends carefully....You reveal your character not only by the company you keep, but by the company you avoid.*

Anonymous

Did you ever hear your mother or father tell you to "Choose your friends wisely?" I'm almost certain you have. When this happens, you might wonder "What's so important about choosing friends, "or "Why don't my parents trust my judgment?"

Well, it's not quite that simple. Your parents or caregivers most likely made some mistakes in this area when they were teens, and they don't want you to repeat their mistakes.

Also, they understand that young people – no matter how smart or talented they are – have a limited set of experiences in life, and often operate from emotion rather than reason. But most importantly, your parents understand just how influential friends can be.

For example, if a stranger in a restaurant suggests that you try a new type of food, you might not take her suggestion seriously…After all you don't even know this person, right? But let's suppose your good friend suggests the same thing. You still may not try the new food, but you would be more open to the suggestion wouldn't you?

Your friends can help to influence the decisions you make, things you do, places you go and how you spend your time. They can influence what things are important or less important to you. They also have an impact on the things you believe, your habits, and your self-confidence. This influence goes in both directions. Your friends can influence you in either positive or negative ways (Remember the chapter on peer pressure?)

For these reasons, it is unbelievably important that you *choose your friends wisely!* This chapter will help you determine the qualities of a real friend so that you can surround yourself with people that *positively* affect you (the information here also applies to girlfriends or boyfriends, by the way).

Did you know that many studies suggest that you can actually evaluate a person based partly on their friends? As one proverb states: "Tell me who your friends are, and I'll tell you who YOU are."


What exactly is a friend? There are so many ways to answer this. The chart on the next page gives some qualities of a true friend....

Since no one is perfect, your friends won't always be, either. You will sometimes argue with your friends. Sometimes you will disagree about things. Even friends sometimes have conflicts. But if someone is your friend, you shouldn't find yourself arguing with them often.

You might have a friend who seems completely different from you in terms of their personality. You are quiet and shy, she is outgoing; you like to read novels, he likes comic books; she likes to watch Oprah, you love CSI. You play chess, she loves video games. He is Muslim, you are Christian. There's nothing wrong with making friendships with people who are different from you or with whom you sometimes disagree.

This is normal. Actually, such differences sometimes make for a wonderful friendship because you both learn from each other and are fascinated by your differences.

The only time that differences become a problem is when one or both of you fail to respect those differences, or think you are better because of them. I have friends with various religious beliefs, political views, professions and personal interests. We've sometimes disagreed on things and even argued, but for the most part, we value our friendships because we learn from each other, support each other, respect each other, do positive things together, and have fun with each other.

Some young people I've taught or worked with seem to have difficulty in choosing good friends. **You** might have challenges doing this as well. So from now on, when you're trying to determine if someone is really your friend, ask yourself the following questions:

1. How does this person usually make me feel? Do I feel confident, safe, respected and accepted in his or her presence, or do I feel the opposite of these things?

2. Do I usually feel energized and hopeful around this person, or drained and depressed?

3. Does this person attempt to put me in situations where I learn, have (healthy) fun, and feel supported?

4. Am I constantly arguing with this person, or do we have harmony between us most of the time?

5. Is this person always competing with me?

6. Does this person generally respect my values and my opinions?

7. Can I trust this person and share my secrets with him or her?

As I stated before, your friends – just like yourself – are not perfect. Everyone makes mistakes and bad decisions. But most of the time, your friend is a positive influence that respects you, accepts you, and wants the best for you. Just think about the "friends" you have now, read the chart on the next page, and determine where each person ranks.

| A FRIEND: |
|---|
| Wants for you what they want for themselves |
| Sees your victory as their victory, and your loss as their loss |
| Is honest; she will tell you the truth even if it upsets or disturbs you |
| Brings out the best in you |
| Doesn't encourage you to violate your values |
| Respects your beliefs, values, and opinions, even if different from their own |
| Is unselfish; she does nice things without seeking something in return |
| Doesn't try to outdo you, or embarrass you, or manipulate you |
| Is someone in whom you can confide |
| Does not get you in trouble with parents, teachers or police officers |
| Sees himself as your teammate or partner |

But what about your other peers in school, on the block or on your team who do not fit the criteria of being your friend? How do you deal with them? People that routinely do the opposite of a person on the chart above are bad news! Such people will get you into dangerous situations, ruin your reputation, get you into trouble with your parents, teachers, or police officers and lead you to compromise your values.

Who wants to befriend someone who is dishonest, disrespectful, insincere, and controlling? Once you determine someone fits any of these categories, you should avoid unnecessary contact with them. By avoiding them, you will also avoid all the trouble and bad feelings they cause.

In conclusion, please remember that of all your decisions, choosing friends will be one of the most important throughout your life. Therefore, CHOOSE WISELY!

## BIG IDEAS

- Your friends have tremendous influence upon you and your development. Often times, you may spend more time with them than members of your own family. Therefore, you cannot afford to choose friends lightly.

- Attending the same school, playing on the same team, or living in the same neighborhood are not factors that should determine who your friends are. You must consider more important things like how the person makes you feel, how he/she treats you, and whether the person is trustworthy, supportive and a positive influence. You should use these same guidelines concerning girlfriends and boyfriends.

## CONCLUSION

We've reached the end of our journey together, and I applaud you for time, energy, and attention. If you carefully read this book, and really thought about the information provided, then you have learned many important things that can make your life more successful and satisfying.

I've done my best to write this book using simple and direct language. If I accomplished this, you might have found it difficult to put this book down. You might have even finished reading in a day or two. That's great! But reading this book once or twice and locking it away in your closet will not help you.

Reading the book was the first part, but your job isn't done yet. Now you need to: think seriously about what you've learned here, discuss these ideas with your friends/parents, and **put these ideas into practice**!

No great building, movement, invention, song, career or person is created overnight. So you may need to read this book several times until you really absorb the ideas. Months after you finished reading you might be going through something and need to revisit a particular chapter or two to help you make sense of things. And even if you completely understand all of the ideas we discussed, it may still take you some time to incorporate the ideas in this book. But stay focused and watch how the quality of your life improves!

Just as nothing great occurs overnight, nothing great occurs without conflicts and mistakes. Real life is full of betrayals, disappointments, detours and problems. No one avoids these things. But with the right skills (like those discussed in this book) you can properly respond to problems and even use them to your advantage.

There are forces in this world that see young people as a generation of "nothin' muffins," or failures in the making. Generally speaking, nothin' muffins:

- Talk loudly but have little of importance to say

- Know how to have a good time, but accomplish nothing of importance in their lives.

- Have no plan for their lives, so they drift around with no sense of purpose like feathers in the wind

- Spend most of their time and money entertaining rather than educating and empowering themselves

- Would rather complain about problems than solve them

- Work their entire lives making other people rich and powerful, but have no such plan for their own families and communities

- Are comfortable with doing just enough work to get by, rather than aiming for excellence.

I wrote this book so that you would **NOT** be a nothin' muffin! I'm expecting you to use this book to be better and do better, both in and outside of class. The future of the United States and other nations throughout the world depend on generations of leaders and problem-solvers like you. Thank you for reading this book, and please spread the word!

As an added bonus, I'd like to leave you with 20 life lessons that will help you way into your adult years. By the way, I'm interested in hearing your thoughts about this book and your suggestions for future editions. I hope you will email me (truself143@gmail.com) and share your thoughts!

---

Lesson 1: Don't take people's words or deeds personally. People sometimes speak or act out of turn for a number of reasons that have nothing to do with you: they might have poor health, be experiencing financial difficulty, death in the family, loneliness, insecurity, jealousy, etc. Don't allow the cloudy attitudes of grumpy or unfulfilled individuals to eclipse the sunshine of your spirit!

Lesson 2: Choose friends wisely. True friends support you and advise you when you need it. Avoid jealous, competitive, and negative types. You want friends that add on to your life, not those who will subtract and divide. Choose friends based on shared values and interests, not simply because they live in your neighborhood or attend your school.

Lesson 3: Do not gossip, and be suspicious of people that do. Speak favorably about a person's strengths in public. Keep your critiques about them to yourself. Do not be naive. Assume that someone will repeat what you say. Gossip causes division and distrust. A sweet tongue can heal wounds or inspire people. A bitter tongue can lead to your destruction or that of others.

Lesson 4: Keep your mind open to learn from everything and everyone. Don't be the type that's quick to say, I KNOW THAT, before the person is done speaking. Even if you know a lot about a topic, you might gain a new perspective by simply listening. Be open to new ideas and perspectives.

Lesson 5: While you are expected to demonstrate humility and respect toward others, you should not worship or allow yourself to be mistreated, degraded, or intimidated by anyone!

Lesson 6: Secure yourself. Your happiness, financial stability, and contentment are YOUR responsibilities. Do not expect everyone to support you, and do not blame others for your problems.

Lesson 7: Do not allow unqualified people to advise you. The world is filled with fake experts and false prophets. How can someone that has never done something for example, advise you on how to do it? When you seek advice from others, make sure they have the experience or knowledge to offer the advice or expertise you need. Otherwise, you will be lost and confused.

Lesson 8: You are so much greater than a mere job. You have with a specific mission to fulfill! Determine what your mission is: why you were put on this Earth, and stay on your path. Everything else will fall in place. How do you discover your mission? Identify what you love to do, what you think about all the time, what you're good at doing, and what brings you peace and fulfillment...

Lesson 9: Spend absolutely NO time concerned about who likes you. Popularity is overrated. You will never please everyone, nor should you even try. There will be people in your class, on your job, in your neighborhood, etc. that will pretend to be cool with you, but secretly despise you and speak ill of you. Stay on your path, be successful, and avoid the haters!

Lesson 10: Treat time like money-budget and use it wisely! In the game of life, there are no timeouts. Organize your life and cut down on idle time by scheduling work, meditation, rest, and recreation. Fools waste time, wise people invest it...

Lesson 11: Life, like the game of chess, is a culmination of choices. To be successful and fulfilled, you must master the art of making good decisions. You cannot float around like a feather in the wind. Be strategic; plan the life you want with wise decisions and actions then implement your plan.

Lesson 12: Always consider yourself a work in progress. Strive for excellence in all you do, but allow room for mistakes and poor choices. Learn lessons from your mistakes, don't fall apart! Meet goals and set new ones; assess your strengths and shortcomings. Perfection is elusive, but excellence and progress are attainable...

Lesson 13: Problems are meant to be solved, not complained or whined about. Endless complaints don't solve your problem. Whining also causes you to dismiss and ignore your blessings. Remember the Chinese proverb: "It is better to light a candle than it is to curse the darkness."

Lesson 14: Approach everyone and everything with confidence. Speak clearly and with authority, and walk with purpose. The world holds nothing but rejection and disappointment for the timid, insecure, and foolish...

Lesson 15: Command the respect of others through your service and contributions. Some may hate Henry Ford, but they still drive cars; others may dislike Floyd Mayweather or Beyonce, but they have to respect their accomplishments. Be so useful, indispensable, and productive, that even your enemies are forced to respect you!!

Lesson 16: Keep your mind's GPS on and working. You will encounter many obstacles, detours, and mishaps as you navigate through life. Distractions and diversions will always be present, threatening to get you off course. Keep your GPS on...make sure that at all times, you know where you are, where you're going, and effective travel routes. *Don't allow anyone or anything to take you off course.*

Lesson 17: Identify and develop mentors. True success comes from collective, not individual effort. Save years of wasted time and effort by learning from mentors (older people that have achieved success in the field or endeavor you like. They will help you cultivate the skills and habits you need to succeed, and will introduce you to important people and opportunities.

Lesson 18: Define your own reality. You are unique. Your very genetic code, you DNA is so unique that no one in world history had it before, no one else has it now, and no one else will have it in the future! It is shameful to see people living their lives according to everyone else's rules and opinions. Dare to define your own expectations, and standards of beauty, success, health, spirituality, etc. Place your unique, distinct footprints in the sand of time

Lesson 19: Live a monumental life. Not only should your life have meaning and purpose for yourself, but for those that come after you. Egyptian pyramids are monumental in size, but the true significance of their greatness is that they are 5-10,000 years old! At every job, school, place of employment, and certainly within your family, leave something behind that will serve others long after you're gone.

Lesson 20: Maintain balance in your life. Fitness is not just physical, but financial, spiritual, political, mental, etc. Strive to be a well-adjusted, diverse, complete human being with a variety of skills, interests, friends, and experiences.

# PART II

# For Parents

## THE WIZARD OF OZ SYNDROME

I am a huge fan of movies and music. In fact, I often think in terms of movies scenes or songs. Far from simply being a form of entertainment, the best art arranges symbols, words, and ideas in ways that inspire and educate us. Bear with me then, as I take you on a journey to explore the larger themes in the famous movie, "The Wizard of Oz."

## Problems Facing Young People

If I asked a room of people to list the problems facing our youth, most could easily do so. Many of us know the *whats*, but we must have serious discussions around the *whys* and *hows*. I will address the issue of how young people can understand and change their negative attitudes and behaviors, and I will use the famous "Wizard of Oz" movie as my primary reference. I know you might believe I'm crazy, but again, just bear with me.

Let me begin by suggesting that this is not your typical children's movie. "Oz" contains symbols, actions, and truths we can use to understand the problems our youth face in society. Several years have passed since some of you viewed this movie, so we'll begin with a summary of the characters and plot:

## Summary of Movie

- Dorothy (the main character) finds herself in a new and strange place far away from her home, after she gets swept away by a tornado

• She meets up with three main characters who like her, have a serious problem

• They are told to follow the yellow-brick road to a city called "Oz" where they will find the all-powerful and wise "Wizard" who can solve their problems

• The "Wicked Witch of the West", threatened by their unity and quest for empowerment, sends several traps/obstacles their way to sabotage their progress

• They eventually meet the Wizard and learn some powerful things about him and themselves

## UNDERSTANDING THE CHARACTERS & THEIR PROBLEMS

When most people saw this movie, they probably did not appreciate many of the themes and symbols presented. We can begin with the four main characters in the "Wizard of Oz. Each character represents a type of person with a specific problem. Examine the chart on the next page:

| Character | His/Her Problem | What the problem Represents |
|---|---|---|
| Dorothy | Away from home and can't get back | Being lost, confused, and disconnected from spirituality, history and culture |
| The Scarecrow | Has no brain | Lack of intelligence and capability |
| The Lion | Has no courage | Low self-esteem, lack of confidence, failure to claim authority |
| The Tin Man | Has no heart | Being insensitive, lacking compassion and humanity |

We can think of these characters as being types of people. One believes himself unintelligent and not capable of thinking. Another lacks self-esteem and authority, and another is ruthless, heartless, and unfeeling. Sound familiar? When you add all these qualities together, you get Dorothy, a person that is LOST!

I submit that the problems we see in our young people stem from these same factors. They are victims of a society (and in some cases *parenting and educational systems*) that teach them they are not capable, not worthy, and destined for lives of failure. With thinking like this, we can understand why they display some of the symptoms we see, right?

## POPPY FIELDS

The Wicked Witch of the West observes the actions of our characters from a great distance. How can she do this? She uses a crystal ball, of course. In real life, people spy on our youth using cameras, satellites, and surveillance devices.

The witch does not like to see these characters unite and seek empowerment. Looking to sabotage their agenda, the witch sends them through a Poppy field, causing most of them to fall asleep.

But what is the significance of Poppy plants? Why do they cause characters to sleep? What does this mean? Poppy plants are used to produce Heroin, Opium, and Morphine, three powerful narcotic drugs. Interesting when you consider how Black and Brown communities were sent through similar "poppy fields" in the 60s, 70s and 80s. Just think about the Heroin, Cocaine, and Crack epidemics in our neighborhoods and all the organizations and families "put to sleep" (destroyed) by them. People addicted to drugs, whose only desire it to get "high" are in no position to fight for empowerment, are they? The Wicked Witch of the West is alive and well, it would appear....

## About the "Wizard"

Our characters manage to stay together and overcome all the obstacles thrown their way. They finally meet the "Wonderful Wizard" who supposedly has the power to resolve each of their problems. The only problem is he is a fake wizard. Quite simply, he is an ordinary man using gadgets and propaganda to make himself seem all-powerful and superior.....sound familiar?

Naturally Dorothy and her friends are upset upon learning the wizard is a fake. They invested so much time, travel and energy to reach him. In fear of his life, and to pacify the people who are now ready to revolt, the Wizard gives them mere *symbols* of the intelligence, courage/leadership, heart/humanity they seek. At this point, we learn that they already possessed the qualities they sought all along!

Interestingly, the "Wizard" gives them a diploma, medal, and award to symbolize the qualities they believe themselves lacking. Hence two lies materialize: One, that they were deficient in the first place, and two, that they magically obtained certain qualities once the wizard validated them. See how this works?

## BRINGING IT ALL TOGETHER

•This society and its institutions work to turn our youth into The Lion (no courage or self-esteem), The Scarecrow (no intelligence or capability), and The Tin Man (Insensitive, impolite, dangerous). When you add all of these qualities together you have Dorothy (someone who is lost, confused, and disconnected from God and culture)

• Our youth are often steered into "poppy fields" to sabotage their progress (drugs, incarceration, gangs, dropping out of school, etc.)

• Our youth are taught to believe not in the authority of God, or themselves, but of men and women who set themselves up as false gods

## How Can Parents Help to Resolve These Problems?

• Provide your children with a strong spiritual foundation so they don't bow down to false gods, or wicked witches!

• Create opportunities for your children to develop a sense of <u>genuine and earned</u> achievement and accomplishment

• Imbue your children with knowledge of their ancestors, culture, and history ("There's no place like home")

• Teach character development. Our world is over-run by vain, arrogant, and selfish people. We must raise children who are useful, **compassionate, and qualified**

• Teach your children to be leaders and problem-solvers, not followers and whiners; create opportunities for them to develop and utilize these skills

- Make education and self-improvement *non-negotiable (mandatory)* in your household

- Connect them to "good witches," or mentors that care about them and will guide them to success

# THE EDUCATION OF BLACK AND BROWN CHILDREN

Many educators, parents, political pundits and school administrators grapple with the issue of providing adequate education to this nation's most vulnerable and underserved citizens: children of color. But while some of us desire to empower and liberate this demographic through education and prepare future generations of leaders and problem-solvers, others have a more nefarious agenda. This agenda disguises itself behind noble-sounding platitudes. Its proponents are conservative and liberal politicians, think tanks, business leaders, educational scholars, and school leaders. Some have malicious intentions, and others have adopted policies without truly understanding their implications or negative intent.

While people of color and well-meaning liberal whites comprise much of this last group, some of them also enter the discussion with negative assumptions about Black and Brown students and the larger communities that nurture them. Indeed, some of you reading this have been seduced into supporting (or at least not opposing) this agenda.

Some people (I am one of them) argue that *the stated agenda of education reform in this country is dishonest, and that the real agenda involves leaving our children behind and preparing them to be members of a permanent underclass.*

Is this true? Maybe this is just speculation and the opinion of conspiracy theory crackpots. Perhaps we'll never know. What we do know is that the social control of Black people via education has deep roots in the United States. In fact we can trace these roots to the turn of the 20th Century, when America was on its way to becoming an industrial power, and Black people were only 4 decades removed from chattel slavery.

James Anderson in his book, *The Education of Blacks in the South*, chronicles how white liberal reformers, business people and white supremacists alike, participated in a great debate around the question of whether Blacks should receive education and what the scope and objectives of that education should be.

These groups held a series of educational conferences to debate these matters. The Capon Springs Conference for Christian Education in the South, convened in 1898 in West Virginia and met two more times in 1899 and 1900.

From these proceedings the Southern Education Board and General Education Board formed. Oil tycoon John D. Rockefeller founded the latter board, which like its southern counterpart, sought to advocate for public education with a special and limited role for Black people.

You will soon see that while some participants were more malicious than others, most of them viewed Blacks as inferior to whites, and ALL of them saw education as a means to control Black labor and constrain Black political empowerment.

Southern white planters, who held rigidly racist assumptions of Black people, believed that Blacks shouldn't receive any education at all. They rationalized that education wasn't necessary for servants and field hands. Additionally they feared Blacks would demand higher wages, political empowerment and generally better treatment if they acquired education.

The northern philanthropists and liberal southern whites responded by arguing that education could be used as social conditioning. That is, the "*right*" education could result in a semi-skilled Black labor force that accepted its place on the bottom of society and would do so *without protest*. Carter G. Woodson implies this in his classic, The Miseducation of the Negro:

*When you control a man's thinking you do not have to worry about his actions. You do not have to tell him not to stand here or go yonder. He will find his 'proper place' and will stay in it. You do not need to send him to the back door. He will go without being told. In fact, if there is no back door, he will cut one for his special benefit. His education makes it necessary.*

During the 19th century Horace Mann, long considered the "Father of American public education" and a strong opponent of African enslavement, advocated a free public education for all citizens. He saw education as an egalitarian means of providing a common and unifying experience for all children. He believed a solid public education would serve to empower and equip citizens regardless of race, religion or origin.

However by the 20th century, corporate barons abandoned Mann's noble vision, choosing instead to use education to maintain and strengthen racial and economic divisions in the United States.

From 1868-1915, the northern businessmen and southern liberal school reformers became strong advocates of Samuel Armstrong's Hampton University model of education for Black people. Armstrong believed Black people were morally corrupt, unfit for leadership or political power, and in need of "civilization."

His curriculum of education for Black people reflected these negative assumptions. Hampton University emphasized rigorous instruction in social etiquette, hygiene, moral instruction, menial labor and a policy of being complacent and disinterested in political and social empowerment. Armstrong was Booker T. Washington's mentor and Washington adopted his educational policies at Tuskegee Institute. Interestingly, Anderson reports that most graduates of these institutions acquired the equivalent of a 10th grade education and received little actual instruction in skills they could leverage into work.

We can see why W.E.B. DuBois mounted such fierce opposition to these agricultural and technical schools and their agenda of social control for Black people. In his classic book *The Souls of Black Folk*, Dubois asked, "Is it possible, and probable, that nine millions of men can make effective progress in economic lines if they are deprived of political rights, made a servile caste, and allowed only the most meager chance for developing their exceptional men?"

DuBois argued that the mode of education championed by Armstrong and Washington would lead to three negative outcomes:

1. The disfranchisement of the Negro (no voting rights).

2. The legal creation of a distinct status of civil inferiority for the Negro.

3. The steady withdrawal of aid from institutions for the higher training of the Negro.

Perhaps the social control agenda of educational reformers exposed by DuBois and Woodson is still in effect today in the 21st century. Moreover, some critics argue that many of today's educational reformers have agendas for and assumptions of Black students that bear a striking resemblance to the 20$^{th}$ century philanthropists and school reformers I mentioned earlier.

In fact, quite a few of the charter school networks we see today were founded by rich and conservative businessmen. These individuals and foundations infuse billions of dollars into school reform and public policy. And they concentrate their efforts in urban areas with majority Black and Brown populations: Albany, Atlanta, Boston, Chicago, Denver, Detroit, Harlem and the Bronx, New York, Indianapolis, Los Angeles, Memphis, Milwaukee, Minneapolis, New Orleans, Newark (NJ), Maryland, and Washington, D.C.

Research into the previous activities of these people and their corporations often demonstrate no evidence of concern for people of color or poor people. In fact, such corporations are often *predatory* (they pay workers significantly below the national average, deny them benefits, and fiercely work to crush union organizing).

Yet, some of these same corporate chiefs with track records of displacing and exploiting workers denying benefits, and placing profit margins over people, suddenly are creating schools in this nation's poorest and most neglected communities. Interesting, isn't it? Perhaps they've experienced a change of heart. Or perhaps they've discovered that there are millions of dollars to make and future cheap laborers to develop in the education *industry*.

And let's not forget the rise of teacher-training programs. In the mid-80s and 90s American public schools faced serious personnel issues. Large numbers of teachers and principals neared retirement or switched careers due to salary and safety concerns. Education boards around the country needed to quickly replace thousands of out-going teachers.

Programs that could help cities replenish these depleting pools of teachers would profit greatly by meeting this need. This was especially true in chronically low-performing urban school districts entitled to millions of dollars in "Title One" funds. Naturally, observant people responded to these circumstances with the creation of teacher-training programs across the country.

Recruits for some of these teacher-training programs are often young white college graduates who did not originally want to be teachers. These recruits undergo a five to eight-week crash course training program to become teachers in America's urban school districts.

Some of these training programs - which are already rushed and incomplete – have a host of problems. They often promote the use of harsh disciplinary measures and "classroom management" techniques more than effective teaching.

When we observe the primary backgrounds of most recruits, with the heavy-handed disciplinary techniques employed by such programs and the neighborhoods targeted, we can't help but wonder if any white paternalism is at play.

Certainly we must question the agenda behind targeting communities of color, why so few of the teacher recruits are people of color themselves, or why more isn't done to select recruits with a strong understanding of and sensitivity to the people of color they will serve.

Given the history of Black and Brown education in the United States, it stands to reason that certain charter schools themselves might form a pivotal part of a social conditioning agenda for people of color.

Throughout the nation, we hear reports of parents and educators protesting how some charter schools employ inhumane disciplinary practices, while robbing teachers of union backing and academic freedom.

In addition, many charter schools provide inadequate services for children with special needs and tend to quickly expel such children or treat them as incorrigible delinquents. They receive tax payer's dollars, in addition to private funding and very little outside regulation. Because they receive public funding, they tend to siphon off money that goes to traditional public schools, leading public schools to close all over the country. Their obsession with test scores and scripted teaching methods robs the joy of learning from our children, whose spirits are often crushed as military-like discipline and an obsession with test scores takes precedence over learning and creative problem-solving.

The products of such educational methodology might well be docile, semi-skilled laborers who stay in their place and remain disconnected from the indigenous communities that produced them. Could this be the agenda of educating Black, Brown and poor children? Do corporate bosses want to produce effective workers for *their* corporations who accept minimum wages, no union backing, and who will not stand up or speak out against racial, gender, and labor exploitation?

As you see, a great deal rides on what school you choose for your children and the seriousness with which you prepare your children to be workers, leaders, and problem-solvers. Our young people are entitled to a quality education with competent and supportive teachers who demand excellence from them and treat them with respect and love. No more, and no less.

This does not suggest that all schools are bad or that all educators and administrators devalue our youth. Through research you will come across some excellent educational choices comprised of independent Afrocentric schools, Catholic or parochial schools, traditional public schools, charter schools, and home-based schools.

Unfortunately, you will also find that truly excellent schools are far outnumbered by mediocre or even failing schools. Also, those excellent schools tend to be selective, highly competitive, sometimes pricey, and unable to accommodate all families seeking to educate their children. And since no school is perfect by every standard, even the better schools may fall short in certain areas including class size, race or gender sensitivity and diversity, culturally inclusive curriculums, humane and fair discipline policies, etc.

Consequently, regardless of what school you choose for your child(ren), you will need to take an active part in your child's education, and not leave this task exclusively to the whims of education scholars, city or state education boards, school administrators, or teachers. It does "Take a village to raise a child," and you will need to take advantage of all your village (community) offers regarding your child's academic preparation and character development.

# 13

## EXPANDING OUR THINKING ABOUT PARENTING

I am no perfect parent by *ANY* means. Some of my reflections about parenting that you're about to read come after years of hindsight thinking about things I could have done better. Nonetheless, I hope to challenge you to rethink and retool your method and philosophy of parenting, as it remains one of the most influential and impacting roles in our society.

Of all the responsibilities one can have, parenting perhaps is the most challenging. It comes with no standard job description or training manual, and requires executing dozens of diverse roles: teacher, counselor, conflict mediator, nutritionist, chef, motivational speaker, dean of discipline, publicist, financial planner, nurse, psychologist, comedian, spiritual guide, tour guide, etc.

Parents play a major role in developing well-adjusted and empowered communities, as individuals constitute communities and parents develop individuals.

This remains true despite the increasing (and often negative) influences of mass media and popular culture. No amount of misogynist songs, questionable fashion trends, low-performing schools, or questionable values can completely sabotage good and consistent parenting.

The problem of course is that while it's easy to become a parent, this alone does not make one qualified to be a good one. And if we are honest, we will concede that not everyone meets the qualifications to be a good parent. In fact, some people that are parents probably should not be. Such an important role is challenging for mature and financially sound adults, and even more so for millions of young, unseasoned and immature youth with scant wisdom, education or financial stability to their credit.

And yet, once we make the decision to have children, the deal is done, leaving us and the larger society to deal with our choice for better or worse. As a former schoolteacher and youth development worker, I've seen firsthand both the transcending power and impact of good parents and the sad and dysfunctional effects of poor ones.

In any case, we are all affected since we inherit both deprived and well-guided children in the form of students, co-workers, love interests, and fellow citizens of the world. Parents wield much more potential power than we give you credit for and it is my aim here to address themes to help you use this power effectively.

## THE ROLE OF PARENTS – MUNICIPAL VIEW

What is the role of a parent? According to municipal law a parent is expected to provide adequate food, clothing, shelter, safety and education for their child. Larger society however, only imposes mandatory minimums or basic standards and expectations on parents. Those unable or unwilling to meet these basic standards risk fines, imprisonment, or having their children taken from them and dispersed to group or foster homes.

## The Social Costs of Poor Parenting

Our local governing bodies take these matters seriously because children of abusive or negligent parents often become societal burdens in the form of being unemployable, dependent on social services, and even involved in criminal activity. In each unfortunate case, taxpayers shoulder the financial burden in an already fragile economy.

## A Broader View of Parenting

Moving away now from the municipal perspective, how do we view our role as parents? I've asked this question and heard a number of varied responses. On the more basic end of the spectrum, parents view their job as providing the basic necessities of life and helping to make their child a "good" person. More sophisticated views include providing children with spiritual grounding, character development and helping children to navigate the bumpy road of life.

These are all noble aims, and I'd like to think all parents count these among their intentions. But perhaps there is room to expand this thinking by approaching it from a different perspective and developing a general outline to effectively reach these objectives.

Instead of raising our children with the guiding idea that they belong to us, how would our parenting improve if we raised our children as individuals that belong to others and to society-at-large?

For example, imagine how our methods and guidance would alter if we thought, "I want to raise a child that will make mature decisions, exhibit good character, and be useful as a student, co-worker/business owner, lover/spouse, community leader, neighbor, friend and parent." Without specifying a long list of tactics, lessons, and activities, just this perspective alone points us in a different parental direction, doesn't it?

This thinking radically broadens our sense of parenthood and makes it more consistent with our social reality. No one lives in isolation from others, so although our child "belongs" to us, in a larger sense, they also belong to the world into which they are born and therefore we must prepare them accordingly. This approach also coincides with the Ghanaian proverb suggesting that "It takes a village to raise a child," since no one household has the total resources, information or energy to provide a child with everything they need to become self-sustaining and empowered.

Indeed, raising children adequately requires collaboration with teachers, spiritual leaders, community leaders and other outside resources. We might consider this a slow, gradual and generational means of social change, transforming our institutions, relationships, and conditions one child and household at a time.

# 14

## UNLOCKING YOUR CHILD'S INTELLIGENCE AND ABILITY

As you know, our increasingly technical world demands workers and leaders who are intelligent, creative and competent problem-solvers. The goal of this chapter is to briefly introduce you to the concept of "intelligence," show you how this concept has changed over the years, and give you tips on how you can unlock your child's intelligence and ability.

For centuries in the United States, we thought of

intelligence in three very limited ways. Generally speaking, intelligence was understood as one's ability to:

Understand and use ideas and language, solve mathematical problems, and analyze and implement information.

> **DID YOU KNOW?**
>
> A child's willingness and ability to work hard, practice and study are more reliable predictors of their future success than test grades, school grades, or "natural ability.

Over the years, educators found flaws with this way of defining intelligence. For example, this definition:

- Only focuses on people that do well with problem solving, critical thinking, and verbal or written expression.

- Leads children without these abilities to view themselves as unintelligent. This contributes to low self-esteem and poor academic performance.

- Leads teachers and parents to choose activities that fail to address the different ways that children learn.

Then in 1983, Harvard University Professor Howard Gardner challenged our old way of thinking about intelligence. He published a book entitled "*Frames of Mind: the Theory of Multiple Intelligences*," which shocked the world by suggesting that there were at least 7 forms of intelligence!

According to Gardner, these included: verbal/linguistic, musical/rhythmic, visual/spatial, bodily-kinesthetic, logical-mathematical, interpersonal and intrapersonal.

*Visual/Spatial intelligence:* refers to one's ability to "think in pictures," to perceive the visual world accurately, and recreate (or alter) it in the mind or on paper. Painters, interior designers, movie directors, and architects display this form of intelligence.

*Bodily-Kinesthetic intelligence* refers to one's ability to control body motions and handle objects skillfully. Athletes, dancers, actors, and mechanics display this form of intelligence.

*Logical-Mathematical intelligence* refers to one's ability to use reason, logic, and numbers to solve problems. Scientists, mathematicians, engineers, and accountants, display this intelligence.

*Intrapersonal intelligence* refers to one's ability to be deeply aware of and in tune with one's own thoughts, feelings, and desires. Philosophers, psychologists, and researchers use this form of intelligence.

*Interpersonal intelligence* refers to one's ability to relate to and understand the feelings and motivations of other people. Teachers, salespersons, businesspeople, ministers, and politicians display this form of intelligence.

*Verbal-linguistic intelligence* refers to one's ability to understand, arrange, and express words/ideas. Poets, authors, attorneys, teachers, radio show hosts, and politicians tend to use linguistic intelligence.

*Musical/Rhythmic intelligence* refers to one's ability to create, perform, and arrange music. Musicians, singers, and composers, display this form of intelligence.

As you can imagine, this multiple intelligence theory had a large impact on education. For years, parents and educators thought a child to be unintelligent or lacking in talent if they didn't speak well, have a huge vocabulary, or perform well in math. Gardner's theory helped us understand that all children and adults are "intelligent" in different ways, often in more than one area, too. Classroom teachers began to develop lesson plans that involved these different forms of intelligence, in order to address the numerous learning styles of their students.

As a parent or guardian, it is very important to your child's personal and professional happiness that you get with the multiple intelligences program! Children we once thought had little to offer the world, we now realize have much to offer the world, in ways we could never previously imagine. Just think: your son or daughter might be a potential civil rights leader, composer, artist, inventor, writer, scientist, politician, etc.

So what can you do to unlock your child's intelligence and ability?

- Teach your child the discipline and habit of *consistently studying, practicing, and working hard*. Successful people are not born, they are made. There is simply no substitute for constant practice and study. All of the people we idolize and whose achievements we applaud worked hard over many years to arrive at their current level of mastery and success. As the inventor Thomas Edison often said, "Genius is one percent inspiration and ninety-nine percent perspiration."

- Encourage your child to participate in a number of different activities. Expose them to various events and experiences. Provide or direct them to activities and events in which they express interest.

- Try to choose events and activities with your child that allows you to explore and connect several intelligences: drawing, debate, writing, creating a poem, song, or rap, cooking, creating a map, assembling a toy or game, etc.

- Review homework with your child and develop ways to teach those lessons using different methods your child enjoys

- Encourage your child to analyze events and experiences around them

- Encourage your child to try new things and to identify lessons/ideas learned from those activities.

## 9 THINGS WE SHOULDN'T TEACH OUR CHILDREN

"Race doesn't matter." The concept of "race" – that we can accurately determine one's intelligence, ability, habits, attitudes or destiny based on their biological racial designation – is a lie and illusion. One's biology does not determine any of these things which are mostly influenced by culture, observation and education. "Race" may be an illusion; however "racism" is real. It might be more appropriate to teach our children to judge people based on anything but their deeds and actions rather than their race or biological characteristics. At the same time, we must teach them that racism/sexism/class exploitation, and the brutality, prejudice, discrimination and injustice that accompanies them, *does exist*, and works in the interests of certain people. Lastly, we should prepare them to identify and challenge these societal vices.

**"Money is the root of all evil."** In fact, money is a measurement of purchasing power, a tool, and something we need in this system to provide for our basic necessities and luxuries. It is also a symbol of our material wealth. But it is not the root of all evil. The person that created this myth most likely didn't want poor people to become wealthy. Ignorance, vanity, greed, competitiveness, selfishness, arrogance, a false sense of entitlement, insecurity, and jealously are far more accurate candidates for being the "roots of all evil."

Given this, perhaps we should teach our children that 1. Money is necessary in our modern economy b. having more of it will provide them with more options in terms of residence, education, food, clothing, entrepreneurship, political power, etc. Therefore they should make plans to acquire money legitimately, budget and invest it wisely, and use it to provide relief to others. But they certainly should not fear, trivialize, or disdain it.

**"Get a good education so you can get a good job."** It is true that a person with a college degree is more likely to earn a million dollars than a person without one. It is also true that a college education is highly regarded as one way to create more career options.

However, the purpose of formal or informal education is not to get a good job, but to primarily develop important contacts/networks, develop successful habits/attitudes, and to learn specific skills/knowledge that will enable a person to effectively pursue his/her goals, improve their community, and fight injustice.

As a secondary consideration, we seek education to acquire the credentials for upward mobility. What one does with these credentials, habits, skills, knowledge and networks is their choice, but we must urge our children to use these resources to understand, create, own, run, influence, and control things in their environment. This is the basis of power.

**"Do as I say, not as I do."** Our actions and behaviors are far better teachers than our words. If we want our children to respect us, we must do our best to make our actions consistent with our words. Mixed messages only serve to undermine a solid relationship with our children, and they cause our children to distrust our advice and teaching. Besides, if there is a major difference between what we tell them and what we do, we are in essence, hypocrites anyway, unworthy of respect or emulation.

**"I brought you in this world, and I'll take you out of it."** Sounds strong and authoritative, but this saying is actually self-defeating and counterproductive. As parents, our role is to provide our children with reasonable boundaries, direction, basic necessities, and sound habits and attitudes. It is far more appropriate to take the position that "I brought you in this world, and I will do everything I can to help you navigate it successfully." A good parent should also provide discipline when appropriate, but never be a bully.

**"No matter how disrespectful, irresponsible, and disobedient you are, I will still provide you with gifts to demonstrate my love for you."** Ok, we don't actually say this to our children, but some of us say it through our actions. As parents we are spiritually and legally required to provide food, clothing, shelter, love and education/discipline.

Nowhere is it written that we must provide the very finest or most expensive clothing, gadgets, footwear or gifts. Quality is not always synonymous with brand name or price.

When we fail to acknowledge this, we make our children materialistic and shallow. We also encourage them to feel entitled to things they don't deserve or haven't earned. Overcompensation for parental guilt by purchasing expensive things for our children causes more problems than it solves.

Gifts for our children should first and foremost be practical, useful and in accordance with their demonstrated level of responsibility. If they lost or broke 3 previous cell phones, or spend too much time on the phone, why buy them another phone? If they don't do their chores, misbehave, perform poorly in school, or demonstrate dishonesty, what message do we send by purchasing the toy, game or gadget they beg us for? And even if they do well in all of these areas, why would we purchase them expensive things they don't appreciate, won't take care of, or that cause us serious debt?

Birthdays and holidays like Christmas (if you celebrate them) should be used to reinforce these points. We must not substitute good parenting with gifts or we will create a selfish, materialistic, vain and irresponsible crop of teens and young adults.

**"I see you as my buddy rather than as my child."** This is another thing we teach our children through actions rather than words. When we share inappropriate conversations and practices with our children and neglect to discipline and set boundaries for them in hopes that they'll be our "friend," we compromise the relationship completely.

When this happens they don't take our parental authority very seriously, nor do they learn appropriate versus inappropriate behavior and speech. Certain television shows, movies, books, topics, and behaviors are simply not appropriate for children. Nor should our children be empowered to make certain decisions that they are not qualified or prepared to make.

There should never be a doubt about who the leader(s) of the household are. My mother and I have a wonderful relationship. We can talk about almost anything and we sincerely enjoy one another's company. But I am now a middle-aged man with two daughters. I've worked for over 25 years and have experienced life in various dimensions. When I was a child however, my mother was not afraid to tell me "no," or to restrict my exposure to certain things, set clear boundaries or to discipline me. All of these are characteristics of what we call "good parenting."

**"It's ok for you to have idle time."** Again, this is another thing we might not tell our children but that we might show them. You can actually evaluate a person by observing how they use their time. Being a successful student, spouse, professional, or parent requires that we manage our time and use it effectively. It is our responsibility to help our children succeed in all their endeavors by making them respect and properly utilize their time.

We can do this by teaching them to schedule their time. There should be adequate time for study/homework, chores, recreation, eating, conversation and rest. Of course this schedule should be flexible, but our children should never be allowed to think that vast amounts of idle or unproductive time are okay.

Just think about this: In all the time children may waste speaking on the phone, playing games or staying updated on celebrity gossip, they could learn another language, improve their vocabulary, visit a museum, learn to read and write music/poetry, improve their reading and writing, learn to play a musical instrument, work a part-time job, and even had more fun!

Helping our children to manage and respect time also allows more time for us parents to do things we need and want to do. And yes, this applies to weekends as well as weekdays, although we can establish a much more relaxed weekend schedule. Our children should help set their schedule and it should be written out and placed on the refrigerator and in their bedroom. Apply this properly and watch how creative, informed, talented and well-rounded your child becomes!

I'd like to thank you for taking the time to read this book. I truly hope your child enjoyed it and found it useful and that you did as well. I'm interested in hearing your thoughts about this book and how it has influenced you and your child. I'd also like to get your suggestions for making future editions of this book better. I hope you will email me your thoughts to (truself143@gmail.com).

# ABOUT THE AUTHOR

Agyei Tyehimba is an educator, writer, and activist from Harlem, New York. He is the co-founder of KAPPA Middle School in the Bronx, New York. He has over 20 years experience as a schoolteacher, educator and youth development specialist

Agyei co-wrote the Essence Bestselling memoir *"Game Over: The Rise and Transformation of a Harlem Hustler,"* which was

published by Simon & Schuster in 2007. In 2013, he wrote *"The Blueprint: A BSU Handbook,"* which provides Black college student activists with the skills and information they need to effectively lead Black Student Unions.

A powerful speaker, Mr. Tyehimba has been featured on NY1 News, Huffington Post Live, C-Span and was a commentator in the A&E documentary "The Mayor of Harlem: Alberto 'Alpo' Martinez.

Agyei is a professional consultant providing political advice and direction for Black student organizations, community activist groups, and nonprofits. Agyei earned his Bachelor's degree in sociology from Syracuse University, his Master's degree of Professional Studies in Africana Studies from Cornell University, and his Master of Arts degree in African American Studies from the University of Massachusetts at Amherst. You can read Agyei's blog of social and political commentary at mytruesense.org

## HOW YOU CAN YOU HELP:

1) Post this link to my blog about the book: http://mytruesense.org/2014/04/03/truth-for-our-youth-a-self-empowerment-book-for-teens/

2) Post this link on Facebook or Twitter showing people where they can purchase the book: https://www.createspace.com/4472824 or Amazon.com

3) When you finish reading the book, register for free at Amazon.com. Type "Truth For Our Youth" in the search, click on the picture of my book, and write a review for it.

4) Visit your local public library. Inform the librarian that you'd like him or her to order a few copies of the book (Truth For Our Youth, by Agyei Tyehimba).

5) If you have a teenaged child, purchase the book for him/her. Encourage friends to do the same.

Made in the USA
Lexington, KY
10 October 2014